MW01273584

Power Crisis
The self-destruction of a state Labor Party

Written by former minister and Labor historian Rodney Cavalier, *Power Crisis* is an explosive account of the self-destruction of the New South Wales Labor government, which has seen a turnover of four premiers in five years, and is heading for rejection and even humiliation by voters at the next state election.

While the catalyst was the thwarted attempt to privatise electricity, Cavalier reveals that the real issue is the takeover of Labor by a professional political class without connection to the broader community or the party's traditions. Drawing on history to illuminate the crisis, this book spans the ALP's history from its origins as a party for the workers, the bitter split over conscription in 1916, the triumph of 24 years of unbroken rule and the policy innovation of the Wran era, to the rise of values-free careerism.

Featuring interviews with ex-premiers Iemma and Rees, *Power Crisis* contrasts the current turmoil and self-indulgence with the stability within New South Wales Labor over generations before, and asks, 'What went wrong?'

Rodney Cavalier is a political historian. He was Minister for Education in the Wran and Unsworth governments and writes frequently for the press and in academic publications on politics, the ALP and sport. He remains an active and despairing member of the Labor Party.

Other titles in the Australian Encounters series
(Series editor: Tony Moore)

Tim Soutphommasane
Reclaiming Patriotism: Nation-building for Australian progressives

Milissa Deitz
Watch This Space: The future of Australian journalism

Power Crisis
The self-destruction of a state Labor Party

Rodney Cavalier

CAMBRIDGE UNIVERSITY PRESS
Cambridge, New York, Melbourne, Madrid, Cape Town, Singapore,
São Paulo, Delhi, Dubai, Tokyo, Mexico City

Cambridge University Press
477 Williamstown Road, Port Melbourne, VIC 3207, Australia

Published in the United States of America by Cambridge University Press, New York

www.cambridge.org
Information on this title: www.cambridge.org/9780521138321

First published 2010
Reprinted 2010 (twice)

Designed by Adrian Saunders
Typeset by Aptara Corp.
Printed in Australia by Ligare Pty Ltd

A catalogue record for this publication is available from the British Library

National Library of Australia Cataloguing in Publication data
  Cavalier, R. M. (Rodney Mark), 1948–
  Power crisis : the self destruction of a state labor party / Rodney Cavalier.
  ISBN 9780521138321 (pbk.)
  Australian encounters.
  Includes bibliographical references and index.
  Australian Labor Party. New South Wales Branch.
  Political leadership – Australia.
  New South Wales – Politics and government–2001–
324.29407

ISBN 978-0-521-13832-1 Paperback

You may well ask why I write. And yet my reasons are quite many. For it is not unusual in human beings who have witnessed the sack of a city or the falling to pieces of a people to set down what they have witnessed for the benefit of unknown heirs or of generations infinitely remote; or, if you please, just to get the sight out of their heads.

Ford Maddox Ford, *The Good Soldier* (1915)

To sum up, then, we may say that that system of control from below adopted by the Labour Party from its inception has been proved necessary by the selfish and cowardly opportunism which has distinguished the workers' parliamentary representatives. As against that disruptive force the machinery of checks and controls has succeeded in maintaining the solidarity and identity of the Party through many crises. But when it comes to a question of forcing a Labour Government to give effect to their platform or realise the ideals they have been sent into Parliament to accomplish, the organisation has broken down. Instead of directing and controlling the activities of the parliamentarians once they have got command of the Treasury Benches, Conferences and Executives and Caucus have only been able to produce revolts and splits which have exposed the workers enervated by spoon-feeding from Labour Ministries, to the tender mercies of bitterly capitalistic Governments.

VG Childe, *How Labour Governs* (1923)

I had been wrestling with smoke.

Morris Iemma

To Sally, Millie and Nicholas

Contents

Australian Encounters with the ALP

Series Editor, Tony Moore

This book is not about the pros and cons of electricity privatisation. Its focus is the power crisis within New South Wales Labor politics, manifest in the political demise of Premiers Morris Iemma and Nathan Rees. This story ends as farce with a succession of self-destructing ministers setting the scene for a terrible day of reckoning when the people of New South Wales come to cast their votes. The malaise threatens to undermine good government not just in New South Wales, but in other states and territories, and increasingly the Commonwealth. While journalists have viewed the fall of Iemma through the prism of an old fashioned ideological war between statists and neo-liberals, between unions and government, Rodney Cavalier analyses the root causes of the crisis to explain why government in New South Wales has become a grim game of musical chairs. He reveals a bitter conflict between an elected Labor government and the party that created it.

The failure of Morris Iemma's bid to sell electricity generation is a symptom of the disease. The problem for modern Labor is the hijacking of party and government by a professional political class – operatives on big salaries with minimal life experience or connection to the broader community. Many of the new generation of Labor leaders, who rose from the ranks of numbers men, spin doctors and the campus ganglands of Young Labor, lack the people and communications skills traditionally associated with the noble craft of politics. Instead, those of the new political class are bureaucrats focussed on factional – and increasingly subfactional – loyalty, dispensing and receiving patronage ahead of a lucrative post-political career as private sector lobbyists. For Cavalier it is rich hypocrisy that the ministers who supported electricity privatisation derided the union-dominated party and Annual Conference – the same power bloc to which they owed their careers. Until the fight over privatisation, they had used this union domination to impose government policy on dissenters within the ALP.

For most of the players, the issues are not ideological. These have been power plays of ambition let loose by the absence of belief. Cavalier's thesis is that the new generation of operatives lacked both the skill and the will to persuade the party and unions of the wisdom of privatisation. Hawke and Keating won party support for a suite of reforms, including privatisation of Qantas and the Commonwealth Bank, by consulting, negotiating with and gradually persuading key constituencies, unionists and branch members, and ultimately prevailed. Pragmatic management of relations between an elected government and the ALP allows a Labor government to get on with governing. The proviso is that the government respects and persuades the party. The course of persuasion has a long provenance, initiated by New South Wales Premier William McKell to end the virtual civil war that plunged Labor into crisis in the 1930s. McKell restored Labor's credibility with voters. Cavalier calls this governance the 'McKell Model'. It was a model followed by his successors; New South Wales Labor enjoyed an unprecedented 24 years in office. It underpinned the success of the Wran and Carr Governments and was a guiding principle (often through gritted teeth) for Whitlam, Hawke and Keating.

With a few noble exceptions highlighted in this book, the new political class has neither understanding nor respect for Labor's traditions. This class seems to look forward to the day that Labor governments, state and federal, through public funding and private donations, can dispense with party members altogether. What does this separation of leadership from a grass roots base mean for how Labor governs?

Rodney Cavalier is not an academic. He is that rarer creature in Australia – an intellectual in politics, a man of letters who commands respect as a Labor historian, branch stalwart and party conscience. Some of the chapters in this volume began life as essays written by the author contemporaneously with the events of 2008 and 2009 by using Labor history to predict that a premier would fall. These essays were published in the *Newsletter of the Southern Highlands Branch*, a journal edited by Cavalier for the past 15 years. Its humble title belies its depth of political insight, sense of history and entertaining prose. *Power Crisis* offers no less.

Preface

In July 2005, Bob Carr announced he was standing down as Premier of New South Wales. Succession would fall to the minister in his Cabinet supported by the dominant Right-wing faction of the Labor Party. Events moved swiftly. The party's General Secretary, Mark Arbib, made clear his preference for the then Minister for Health, Morris Iemma, over the supposed favourite, Carl Scully. A phalanx of MPs from the ALP Right proceeded to align their support with the wishes of the General Secretary. The amount of public discussion was minimal, what was done was done in private. It was done quickly. Carl Scully announced his withdrawal from the race. Iemma proceeded to be unopposed within the Right and unopposed within the State Parliamentary Labor Party.

Within days, Deputy Premier Andrew Refshauge and Planning Minister Craig Knowles resigned from the ministry and the Parliament. In a matter of months, the ALP had lost the ticking heart of the Carr government – Carr himself after 24 years in Parliament; Michael Egan, an energetic Treasurer with interests across all policy, who had first entered Parliament in 1978; Refshauge, nominally on the Left, a veteran of 24 years; Craig Knowles, a man of integrity, in his 20th year as an MP, out of contention because of indiscretions sub-trivial.

Any advantage to the Liberal Opposition was forfeit almost instantly. The Liberal leader, John Brogden, was the subject of newspaper reports of his alleged behaviour in bars with women who were not his wife. Amid concerns about breaches of the privacy of a public figure and the ethics of the reportage, Brogden resigned.

The Liberal Party proceeded to elect a new leader of little experience and next to no judgement. Peter Debnam was a gift to Labor of the kind that comes but once per generation. The Liberals had passed over the incumbent deputy, Barry O'Farrell, the standout in their ranks and the one obvious leader. Factionalism in the wider Liberal Party had infected the parliamentary ranks.

At the 2007 state election, the Opposition failed to offer an alternative transport policy. It vested great faith in a policy of recycled water, an issue of no concern for the electorate. The slogan employed by the Iemma government was perfectly pitched – 'More to do but we're heading in the right direction' – a message connecting to market research that found major concerns about the provision of basic services by the government. The same research turned up real fears that the Opposition could not be trusted with government. Labor campaigned counter-intuitively by leaking stories that it could lose.

The result was a triumph for Morris Iemma. The large majority that Carr had won in 1999 and retained in 2003 was essentially intact. The son of Italian immigrants, a boy who had taken days off school to act as interpreter to a father in search of work had become the first Premier since 1959 to have succeeded to the office mid-term and won the election following. He had no enemies of significance in a united party. Morris was a husband and father who delighted in the company of his family. His friends and allies dominated the ALP machine. Within his faction there was not a single credible alternative. A triumphant Labor was daring to believe that it was at the mid-way point of another term of 24 years, a worthy successor to the Labor governments in power in New South Wales from 1941 to 1965.

Within 18 months all was in ruins. The Premier felt compelled to resign after being rebuffed by his faction on plans to reconstruct his Cabinet. The new Premier, elected that day from outside the ranks of the dominant Right, was himself gone after another 15 months. Labor had crashed to ruin because its Cabinet was determined to sell the electricity assets of the state. Electricity privatisation had not been an issue in the 2007 poll. The Premier could not claim a mandate for the course his Cabinet was proposing. That course placed it four-square in collision with the policies of the party that the Cabinet claimed to be representing.

Selling public assets was said to be a public benefit beyond debate. The mainstream media and all the specialist commentators on business and politics predicated their every comment on the certainty that all sales of public assets were good, government getting smaller was good, government getting out of public utilities was good. Labor identities of former prominence endorsed the Iemma government's intentions. New South Wales politics now existed inside a wholly different values system from the one that operated as recently as the Wran era, light-years from the values of the policies of reconstruction that had followed the winning of Second World War and the public spending programs designed to win the peace. In those more enlightened distant days, spending was seen as investment. Plaudits went to builders of public assets. The champions of old Labor were those who extended services to those in need. It was a given to old Labor that government was the instrument. Progressive rates of taxation and judicious borrowings were the means of funding the programs of an interventionist state.

The 1980s turned virtue on its head. Governments had to get out of enterprise. Cutting staff and services won applause. Federal Labor under Bob Hawke and Paul Keating had led the way with the sales of the Commonwealth Bank and Qantas. The Howard government had succeeded in selling Telstra. Fabulous sums resulted from these sales of public assets. Some were parked in sovereign funds, much was spent on ongoing programs and tax cuts for the middle class.

The public enterprises of the Australian states had once built a nation. Now state enterprises were said to stand in the way of economic growth. Most of the business of the states, essential services socially vital, ran at a loss. The great exception was electricity – its generation, transmission and supply. Profits were being made with every transaction. The Kennett government in Victoria had made a motzer by selling the state's electricity assets at the top of the market. Bob Carr and Michael Egan had tried in 1997 and failed. They had not tried again. Eleven years later, Morris Iemma was going to try again. He enjoyed the passionate support of his Treasurer,

Michael Costa, a one-time Trotskyist who had become a disciple of market freedom.

The Premier was prepared to stake his leadership on getting his legislation through. The opponents of sale were prepared to exact that price if that was the price of defeating the sale. The battleground was the forms and structures of the Australian Labor Party. The coming struggle etched how unrepresentative was its governance. What follows is not a laying of blame on union secretaries for acting in the interests of their members. The Rules of the ALP vest control of the party in its affiliated unions, a rump that represents some 8 per cent of the voters of the state. None of the victims of the assertion of union power in 2008 ever had cause to complain about union control when it was delivering what they wanted.

Morris Iemma had fallen as Premier, brought down by his own party after he had sought to defy a decision of the party in conference. Fifteen months later Nathan Rees fell as Premier, brought down by his own party because he had implemented a decision of the party in conference. The Labor Party broke in 2008. It will be a long time before people of goodwill are able to put it back together.

The backdrop to this story is the attempt to privatise electricity, told through concentrating on a number of people central to events. It is an attempt to understand how modern Labor governs. The arc of such a story necessarily omits the impressive achievements of these Labor governments in areas like education, the natural environment and the administration of justice. For any Minister for Education to take his or her portfolio out of the firing line is an achievement. The names of Bob Debus and John Hatzistergos do not enter these pages, yet their accomplishments as Attorneys-General are fine stories of public service. Those and other stories of sound public administration are necessarily lost when the leadership of a government is in crisis unending and all too much that is unsavoury becomes public.

I have built this account out of diaries and conversations held during this succession of crises as they were unfolding. Research for the book caused me to seek interviews with many of the participants. For the first time I listened closely to the architects of the aborted privatisation, why they sought to do what they did and what they thought they were saying as they tried to persuade the Labor Party that sale was essential.

I was confident that I knew this narrative and its arc. Daily reportage was of value only to the extent it revealed the thinking of the ministerial proponents of privatisation. The reporters were enthusiasts in a cause, backed to the hilt by their editorial managers. An explanation of the case against sale did not get an airing.

There was no mystery or nuance about what was driving the government. There was no cause to question the motives of the ministers in the Iemma government: genuinely they believed that privatising the state's electricity assets was driven by economic necessity. The funds released would underwrite the government's social programs.

Essays written for a monthly publication are in a register quite different to the demands of a book. The continuing research into the fall of Morris Iemma became overwhelmed by events as it appeared increasingly likely that the leadership of Nathan Rees would also be toppled no later than early 2010. The drama of the 2009 Annual Conference brought on the end-game and a swift resolution. The end of the Rees leadership brought the scope of this book to a definite end.

I am grateful to the many people inside this story who shared their memories. The nature of factional intrigue is that there is no official record, very few bother with (or endanger themselves with) contemporaneous notes. Such battles are not the stuff of email exchanges, though text messages mobile-to-mobile are very revealing. The more distant from events the more readily participants will share a memory. That participants disagree on the course of events does not mean one or the other is not telling the truth as he or she recalls the past. The speed of events piling one upon another in the course of a crisis does not readily allow for contemporaneous note-taking. Good records of dates and times do anchor a narrative flow and will jog memories in a purposeful way.

To complete the book I spoke to the two former Premiers at length. Morris Iemma enjoys a good and organised memory which he will enunciate in orderly sequence. Nathan Rees, a serving MP, was necessarily less frank about who betrayed him. Others gave extended interviews on the basis that their names would not be revealed. All interviews required phone calls for clarification. The interviewees were remarkably patient in dredging their memories and hunting down notes and records, if they existed.

Acknowledgements

I would like to thank Susan Hanley, Debbie Lee, James Drown and the staff of Cambridge University Press for their interest and valuable advice. I thank Tony Moore who was the first to perceive that a series of essays in the *Newsletter of the Southern Highlands Branch* warranted republishing as a book. Tony did not once doubt that I could perform a task a great deal more difficult than buckling the essays with some connecting sentences.

Michael Samaras, Ken Turner, David Clune and Andrew West have been cajoling me for years to turn my writings into a book. Their enthusiasm at the news that I was having a go has been a solace throughout the prolonged period of research and writing.

Daryl Melham, John Faulkner, David Clune and Graeme Wedderburn read some or all of these pages at various stages in their preparation. Their suggestions were always valuable.

I thank the members of the Southern Highlands Branch for backing the *Newsletter* for 15 years, a thanks that extends to the subscribers beyond the Branch who have funded its considerable expansion. But for the huge body of writing to meet the needs of a monthly journal, I doubt that I could have recaptured the immediacy of feeling in even recent events.

Above all I thank Sally Ray for tolerating the mess this writing has created and for continuing to make most everything possible.

Introduction

Workers in the colony of New South Wales created a political party in reaction to the use by employers of the full might of government to defeat strike action. The year was 1891. Workers had organised themselves into trade unions to protect and enhance the rights and working conditions of their members by way of action in common. Trade unions formed a political party in their own interest by establishing local labour leagues which anyone with a commitment to a party of organised labour could join. The party was a localist party – a labour league for every suburb and town across the colony with sufficient local support.

The party grew from below. The leagues selected their own candidates to contest constituencies in the Labor interest. For the first time in the history of Westminster parliaments, a coherent mass of people without wealth, income, ancestry, property, social standing, patronage or powerful connections could seriously contest the constituencies where they lived. Labor candidates and MPs came from the communities they represented. Having themselves selected a local candidate, all of the members of the leagues united behind that candidate. In return, the candidates selected for the first outing in 1891, for all of the party's first century and beyond, were obliged to express the views of the membership below. Without that right to select their own candidates – the driving imperative for the party's founding – the Labor Party would have been nothing.

Being a member of the Labor Party was highly valued by those who became members. Through that membership, the dispossessed could feel empowered. Members in branches, acting in concert, could advance policy that eventually became law. There was never a golden age of membership involvement. There was, nonetheless, much of a century when ALP members valued their membership and, just as surely, the Labor Party valued its members. Labor governments treated with respect what emerged from below. From below was where all members of Labor governments had once come.

By the 1980s, this relationship had changed. The Labor Party was beginning to hollow out below. Members stopped bothering to renew, those who stuck were growing older. All too many members saw no point in continuing to belong to a party that did not value them. The leaderships of parliamentary parties addressed the problem of this death below by engineering operational independence from the party in whose name they governed. By the 1990s, the hollowing was affecting the life and health of party branches. Between 1999 and 2009, just over one hundred local branches folded. By 2010 membership numbers had fallen below a critical mass, the Labor Party had disappeared from the life of the Australian community. Labor MPs had come to represent a political class which enjoyed no social base beyond its own ranks. The quality of government was necessarily affected by the closing down of all but a narrow pool for future MPs.

This book is not about the case for or against privatising the electricity industry in New South Wales. Both sides were argued in commissioned reports and in the media. This book is about the internal life of the ALP, what remains of it after this dying of the party below and the loss by trade unions of their social relevance. It considers the rules of a party that bind all members, from premiers to the person who joined the party last week. It is a story told through the actions of key players.

At its birth the ALP had established principles of solidarity. The party had always adhered to those principles, sometimes at great electoral cost, down the decades. The party had asserted its prerogative to be involved in the policy-making of Labor governments. Candidates who sought Labor preselection knew those expectations. Labor MPs sought elevation to Cabinet well aware that there was a party beyond Parliament. They understood that policies sketched the expectations of the party and that there were rules which bound them to fulfil the party's expectations, even if, in practice, the implementation and the timetable for implementation were in the gift of Labor governments. Labor premiers accepted that there were restrictions imposed upon them by the party. Premiers had to find their own way through any conflicts between the party and what party leaders reckoned was their obligation to the electorate and the state. Ultimately, after all the deals were done and dusted, the party had to prevail.

Every candidate for election in the Labor interest signs a Pledge, an obligation enforceable by disciplinary machinery established by the Rules. Candidates who sign the Pledge are aware of its reach and the strict obligations imposed upon them. ALP Rules bind every member of the party to support endorsed candidates, regardless of personal disposition. The full resources of the party are committed to electing candidates endorsed by the party. In return, Labor candidates elected to parliament are bound by the Pledge, in writing, to support the party's policies and platform as decided by the party in Annual Conference. For over a century, the wider electorate has voted for or against the ALP in full knowledge of its organisational principles.

In 2008 the Iemma government argued that it had a separate obligation to the electorate – true of all Labor governments – which in the circumstances of the time overrode the Pledge each of its MPs had signed. Ministers relied upon a doctrine of financial necessity, an argument of last resort in which they defined the extent of the problem and pronounced the one and only solution. There was no alternative, argued the government, to the sale of the state-owned electricity industry. Members of that government claimed for themselves a freedom to defy decisions of Conference. Ministers, supported by a majority of Labor MPs, were going to choose when they would set aside the Pledge they had signed. They were daring the party to impose the discipline that the Rules prescribe for such defiance.

The history of the Australian Labor Party in New South Wales – some 117 years by 2008 – had involved previous acts of defiance, always with the same consequence: the offender placed himself or herself outside the party. In 2008, ALP-endorsed MPs, a majority in both houses, asserted that the Pledge bearing their signature was not a binding commitment, not an obligation of honour. As arbiters of their own behaviour, they would do whatever they thought necessary. An even bigger crisis, the like not seen in 92 years, was avoided only because their assertion did not face the ultimate test of a vote on the floor of Parliament.

Chapter 1

New South Wales Labor and its leaders

Competition for power is the natural condition of political activity. At its first electoral outing in 1891, Labor won seats in large numbers – 35 seats on debut, an arrival not matched by the Country Party, One Nation, nor any other political force in all the years since. Seats won and held acquired status as 'safe', impregnable fortresses akin to the property of the party, the most valuable of spoils there for the taking. Or giving. Labor endorsement was tantamount to winning the seat. With payment of MPs and the achievement of government, membership of Parliament via ALP endorsement became an entrée to power and a glittering life. Men would do almost anything to win that prize. So, it has proven, will women.

The people in charge of party administration – and those who challenge them – have believed their pre-eminent task to be the delivering of the prize of Parliament to themselves and their supporters. If the master plan for local preselection required support in the higher levels of the party, the master plan warranted such an amendment. Preselection battles have echoed wider struggles for control of the administration and the right to write the rules of conflict; those wider struggles were preludes to the right to dominate the preselection process. Every serious schismatic struggle in the ALP is about determining who gets to select who goes into Parliament.

The means of choosing the candidate once seemed so straightforward. Given the party came into existence as a vehicle for expressing the will of working people by democratic means, only one approach was possible – a local ballot of the local members of the Labor movement. But what was membership?

The unions affiliated to the party regarded it as their own. Their sense of possession was the product of an indivisible sense of the Labor movement: union members were members of the Labor Leagues; union officials were league officials. The unions exercised hegemony because they imported their pre-history whole and without question to the embryonic party that they had created in their own image. Union members joined the leagues as individuals, mixing with other members who were not and could not be unionists. The ALP acquired a vibrant culture for internal transactions. The unions brought a program of action which long sustained the party's ideology and ideas. The unions at the party's birth did not enjoy a majority at conference. Why would they need their power entrenched when the entire culture of the party was a living expression of union principles of collective action and solidarity carried out by party members who were themselves union members and members of a family whose bread winner was a unionist?

For its first 25 years, the party survived and prospered with the ALP branch membership in unfettered control, unions in an honoured but minority role. The period 1891–1916, the founding decades, is the era of establishment, the creating of Labor Leagues across the state, growing membership, the birth of an entirely new political process. In this era the Labor Party acquired legitimacy. The party in Parliament evolved from being a third force, when it occupied a corner of the Legisaltive Assembly, from which it could negotiate support in exchange for legislation in the interests of working people. By the early 1900s the party was the alternative government, a threat sufficient to cause non-Labor forces to unite to meet the challenge. In 1910 Labor in New South Wales and in the Commonwealth became governments with a majority in their own right.

The union leaders who founded the party understood political reality and the need for maximum effectiveness: they perceived that their creation had to be self-governing. They established the Labor Party at a time when it was unimaginable that there was going to be any separation of personnel between league leadership, union leadership and parliamentary representation. People worked where they lived, they attended league meetings at night with their fellow workers and fellow residents. MPs came from their ranks. They did not expect that MPs would leave them or the towns and suburbs where they lived. The party was always more diverse than the myth that people in employment were its sole stalwarts and pioneers. From its foundations the party attracted small farmers, small shopkeepers, publicans, journalists, reformers who were materially comfortable and intellectuals, as surely as it attracted wire-pullers and ward-heelers in for the take.

Before the 1890s standing political organisations did not exist. In Westminster-based democracies, campaign committees came in and out of existence, inordinate power accrued to grandees. Candidates standing in the interests of family or capital 'emerged', the choices of a narrow base of influence that had ruled Britain and the fledgling Australian colonies. Candidates did not have to be wealthy but they had to be connected. The Labour Leagues provided a new connection, a formalised and official endorsement which soon proved to be the only means of gaining election in a large number of constituencies.

Universal manhood suffrage, achieved in New South Wales for the Legislative Assembly in 1858, made possible a challenge to the old assumptions. Even though the ruling classes did exceedingly well in repelling the challenges through the ballot box, they were compelled to adopt the machinery of the challengers – a standing party organisation with a defined membership and a system of pre-selection so as to determine that only one candidate standing in their interest entered the field.

Australian Labor broke the mould of politics by vesting control in its own membership. Defining membership created a host of irresolvable problems. Instead of birth and self-proclamation determining who was inside the Labor fold, the party established conditions for belonging and conditions for remaining. A physical ticket was the first essential proof of membership. Its printing and issue created a bureaucracy, an organisation based on documents and a retrievable records system. Someone had to keep the files. The Labor Party was not a turn-up-and-go-home-again affair. Chance assembly gave way to duly constituted meetings convened by notice at a time, date and place determined by the membership. The greatest tribute to the success of this internal governance was that all other parties (then and since) have imitated Labor.

Members of the party could and did gather at other times, they might discuss matters of moment and plan activities. A branch meeting was more than just a gathering of party members. A branch meeting was a properly constituted deliberative forum of the party below. A branch meeting enjoyed the status of a meeting of the ALP. That status conferred majesty.

Decisions of a branch meeting entered a minutes book, a marking up of deliberations which accorded those deliberations the full force of the Rules and the democratic assumptions that gave birth to the party below. Converting a motion into a resolution was a matter of moment. Once passed, it was recorded accurately and was the basis for those in authority to advance its text as far as the wider democracy of the party permitted. A second debate would surely ignite if anyone felt the Minutes were less than complete and fully accurate. Branches mattered. Decisions of branches mattered. Recording those decisions accurately mattered.

Branches were high maintenance. They needed officers and standing committees. A president would chair meetings. A secretary

recorded decisions and took responsibility for dispatching corre-
spondence based on those decisions. Fundraising was ongoing, as
was accounting for those funds. Funds under branch control enabled
branches to control local campaigns. Branches elected delegates
to higher party bodies. Questions of party governance became an
ongoing preoccupation.

The branches were known as leagues. They were free assemblies of working people and their supporters. They resolved to keep
meeting. Those present identified themselves as bound to each
other by the issuing and acceptance of membership tickets with
which they could prove their membership to the world and each
other. The leagues acted in concert with other leagues in the local
electorate. They came together once a year, beginning in 1892,
as the Labor Electoral League NSW Annual Conference. The local
leagues conducted their own affairs for the most part, selected their
own candidates and came together to create something akin to a
modern political party when early success in parliamentary elections dictated the need to reach agreement on matters of detail
in policy and platform. Other than when contesting elections, the
leagues were largely self-governing.

If more than one person wanted to be the Labor candidate,
success fell to he who persuaded a majority of the membership
of the leagues in that electorate. Given that the membership was
neither fixed nor permanent, the shortest course to victory became
introducing as many as possible precommitted supporters to the
ranks of formal membership. From its beginning, the struggle for
preselection drove the membership base of the party.

The character of Labor governance

In the 1890s, Labor had to impose solidarity on all of its MPs in
order to extract concessions from other parties. Individual conscience could not be a factor in how a Labor MP cast his vote in the
Parliament and the ethos created tensions within the parliamentary
party from the moment of its birth.

The 35 MPs elected at Labor's first outing in the New South Wales election of 1891 sought to bind each other to take a Pledge which would override their personal views in favour of the collective obligation to vote as one for what a majority resolved. A large number refused and departed Labor's ranks within months of their election. The party had its first serious split inside its first year of operating.

The danger of such governance is that defeat for a minority meant total defeat, even on matters of personal principle, even on matters with an electoral cost in the local constituency. Victory when it is total can be a taste so sweet that hubris becomes a by-product. Defeat when it is total may result in bitterness, a sense of futility, a questioning of the value of ongoing loyalty. Labor's periods of sustained success have coincided with astute management of the party's minorities, shifting or settled, so as to avoid the conclusion that opposition is hopeless.

The ALP was created in the cause of Laborism, the notion that candidates representing the interests of working people and their families would contest free elections with a view to capturing control of the colonial Parliament, its government and instrumentalities. In control, acting as a government responsible to the Parliament and in accordance with the rule of law, Labor governments would use the authority of the state and its spending capacities to protect the interests of working people. Labor governments would direct resources however required to overcome the inequalities experienced by those without wealth and dependent on the earning power of their labour. No less crucial to Laborism is the acceptance that continuation in power depends on free elections and the will of the people. Labor has not been tempted by the Leninist alternative.

Labor has endured all of a passing parade of Trotskyists; the differing dispositions of Moscow to an authorised penetration of the ALP by its own members; the romantic longing of BA Santamaria for a nation of Italian-style villages operating in an agricultural economy. The mainstream of the ALP has accepted as a given the democratic process of parliamentary elections and the right of an elected government to govern. In politics, what is self-evident is taken for granted. The Labor movement did not have to adopt this model, but it did and has not deviated. The factions have all played the game without ever questioning the wider purpose: that game is to maximise influence in and over the parliamentary parties. The self-imposed circumscription of Laborism has meant that the divisions within Labor – as savage as they sometimes were – have been limited to questions of ends not means.

The nature of factions in NSW Labor was shaped from the outset by the immediacy of electoral success, reinforced by the capture of state government in 1910. Electoral prospects alter the compass of internal debate: the policies of a party in serious pursuit of elected office are a matter of moment beyond the ranks of the party. The knowledge of electoral consequence creates fierce conflict between those who advocate a program which will attract sufficient electors to make the party the government and those who believe that certain principles are so central that their violation is more important than any single election. Around these extremes, necessarily caricatures, the party has enjoyed its most fundamental divides.

Resolving these extremes is the essence of what we have come to regard as a good Labor government: the pursuit of executive power by every possible means within the law, power pursued not as an end in itself but in order to implement ALP policy. The historian Bede Nairn in his work *Civilising Capitalism* has chronicled the battle of the 1890s for the wording of the first party platform. The platform of 1896 was built on the premise that it was the basis of a future election victory. Those in Parliament were more cautious than those not there. A grouping that went under the rubric of Socialists wanted more radical measures. They bridled at the slow pace of parliamentary action.

This frustration is well captured by William Holman, a future Premier and future apostate, writing to Billy Hughes, a future Prime Minister and another future apostate: 'If we potter along as we've been doing for the last two years *we*'re done, *you*'re done, *the* cause is done'. Writing in the 1970s about a division of ideology and purpose, Nairn offered a judgement that describes then, describes now, describes all the years in between:

> Sooner or later, some of the socialists would have to decide whether the Party really deserved the time and effort they were putting into it; while the rest, and the majority non-socialists in the leagues, would have to consider whether the minority were too much of an electoral embarrassment to be carried further.

The new political organisation made decisions on organisation and procedure that have defined the party. After an express commitment to socialism at the 1897 conference of leagues, the MPs lobbied for a no less express reversal. While wording so drastic did not come to pass, the commitment was weakened to an extent that made the MPs content. A Socialist Objective has formally bound the ALP since the 1920s without those words providing either guidance or obstacles to Labor in government. By 2010 a Socialist Objective was a scarecrow.

The organisational reforms were critical. Conference voted to place MPs on the State Executive, the Executive became pre-eminent over district assemblies which had previously decided on granting league charters. The Executive became the court of appeal on matters of discipline. Otherwise, the leagues remained self-governing and could select their own candidates (unless fraud against them was proven). The destruction of any semblance of local power or regional power has proceeded ever since and is now triumphant. In the matter of centralising power, the major factions have colluded more often than not.

Conscription: The great dividing line

The year 1916 is the great dividing line in Labor history. The conscription crisis of the Great War smashed Labor to pieces. Supporting conscription was presented by the Labor Prime Minister, William Morris Hughes, and several Labor Premiers, as a question on which the survival of the Empire was at stake. The fundamental issue was whether the Labor Prime Minister and the several Labor Premiers could and should decide the policy of the party. What was being decided was whether this measure, or any other, was a matter which the party in conference would decide and, in deciding, would bind even those as high and mighty as the Labor Prime Minister and the several Labor Premiers. Were some issues so important that Labor governments could do as they wished, regardless of party policy? They were arguing that their duty was to govern in the national interest.

The Labor Prime Minister, Premiers and senior ministers resisted that direction. When the party directed them, they defied that direction. Hughes was expelled by his own league, expelled by his federal electorate council, expelled by the NSW Branch. When he attended the federal Labor Caucus, he was no longer a member of the party in which he held the status of leader. A majority of Caucus refused to back him. Outnumbered, certain to be removed from office, still Prime Minister, no longer Labor leader, the Prime Minister left the Caucus room.

Hughes had been a founder of the Labor Party, a giant beyond peer, the dominant identity of his time. When he left the Caucus room, he left the Labor Party. Those who followed him that day and in the days following, including several Labor Premiers, many MPs and ministers, were all expelled from the party, cast into an outer darkness – never to be forgiven, never again recognised, acknowledged or paid basic courtesies. Men who had been friends for a lifetime, as close as men could be, did not ever again speak to each other. Not a word for for the rest of their lives. Respect for former friendship was too strong for forgiveness ever to be possible. Until in death, in moments of grief beyond the imagining, these former friends attended the funerals of former friends, men they had not ceased to like and admire. They stood on the fringes, beyond the churchyard, separate to the congregation out of respect for the man who had once been their friend.

It was in 1916 that the NSW Annual Conference was captured by a group calling themselves the Industrialists. That capture resulted in new rules for representation at conference that vested majority control in unions affiliated to the ALP. That year, that Conference, is the moment when the membership of the Labor Party ceased to control the party, when control passes to outside forces. Before 1916, the Labor Party was controlled by its members. After 1916, it was under the control of affiliated trade unions, which meant that the party was in the hands of whatever coalition of union officials could command a majority at the Annual Conference. Control of Conference was control of everything: Conference elected the Central Executive (and the equivalent by other names down the decades) and the party officers. The officers ran the party day to day, and employed the authority of the executive at every level of the party across the state. Through the ability to determine disputes, eligibility for voting and intervene in preselections, the party officers exercised effective control over any matter which interested them, including the affairs of the parliamentary party and its leadership. The only limit to the reach of their authority was self-denial or the prospect of intervention by the Federal ALP (which like clockwork intervened in the parlous NSW Branch in 1925, 1940, 1955 and 1970). For the Labor Party, the crisis of Billy Hughes and conscription has never been resolved. Labor has recovered from the Great Split of the 1950s. The party has not recovered from 1916.

Throughout the 1920s, the Labor Party was hostage to the shifting sands of union alliances. The 1930s smashed the lives of Labor's supporters. If governments could get high and mighty, so could those who controlled the ALP. Jack Lang, Labor's NSW leader, twice Premier, harnessed the power of the ALP's machinery to eliminate his opponents in Parliament and beyond. Lang had contrived a reverse takeover whereby, vaunting the authority of a Conference and Central Executive controlled by his liegemen, Lang's interests prevailed in all matters. The leader was elected by Conference. One could neither gain nor retain preselection except by bending the knee to the Big Fella. People of the calibre of Ben Chifley and Ted Theodore preferred defeat to submission. NSW

Labor operated as a separate party within the Federal Parliament for much of the 1930s.

The Lang catastrophe

The 1920s Caucus was seriously weakened by the expulsion of its leader and Premier, William Holman, along with much of the generation who had founded the ALP, for their support of conscription. John Storey – known as 'Honest John' because that quality was so rare in the Labor Party of the time – brought the party back into government immediately after the conscription schism. He might have been the man to provide the leadership required. Storey died young. NSW Labor seemed to heading for a Shakespearian resolution. As men without principle vied for power, the blood shed in each powerplay washed into the next and the next and the next.

The beneficiary of the turmoil was John Thomas Lang. Serious evil will triumph when good men have abandoned the field. Jack Lang is the great scoundrel of NSW Labor politics, his seat in the pantheon not disturbed by romantic notions that some sort of principle motivated his defiance of the Governor in 1932. For the length of Lang's leadership, public division was the custom. Men of goodwill plotted for his downfall almost as soon as he became leader. There were at times two central executives operating inside the ALP, two Labor parties on the floor of the Legislative Assembly. Expulsions became the norm for dissent.

Lang was obsessed with centralising power in his person and within his immediate reach. The Central Executive appointed the parliamentary leader. The Central Executive approached absolute authority when it added the right to select all ALP candidates. Thereafter, serving MPs had to keep on the right side of Lang in order to survive. Or leave Labor and survive on their own.

The Depression demolished governments across the world. Lang was swept to power in 1930 with 55 per cent of the primary vote. For the moment, disdain toward Langism in the country did not much matter. Lang was clueless about economics. He brought New South Wales close to ruin. In the absence of a coherent response,

Lang employed demagoguery against foreign loans. The state was running out of funds. The State Savings Bank collapsed. Lang had killed the federal Labor government by inducing his supporters in the Federal Caucus to support a motion of no confidence in the House of Representatives. Thereafter Lang Labor acted as a distinct fourth party in the Parliament throughout the 1930s. At the federal election that resulted from the treachery of the Lang forces, Labor experienced its worst result in the history of Federal Parliament. Each of Ben Chifley, John Curtin and Ted Theodore was lost from the Parliament – Theodore forever. The ALP lost all but one federal seat in New South Wales; Lang Labor was a key impediment to regaining national office.

Lang met his fate in 1932 when, bent on measures of questionable legality about meeting the funding crisis, he ignored the express warnings of the Governor of New South Wales that the proposed course would result in his dismissal. NSW Labor copped its greatest ever defeat and became well-nigh unelectable. Lang survived only because the Caucus had no say in the leadership. Another defeat was necessary, and another, before the party grasped the courage to deal with Lang. The source of that courage was the utter determination of the federal leader, John Curtin, to overhaul the NSW Branch, coupled with the unending opposition to Lang within the state by a few brave MPs centred on Bob Heffron, a number of unions and the likes of Ben Chifley, who was the NSW President of federal Labor during these wilderness years.

A different governance

In 1891 William John McKell (future Premier of New South Wales) was born in Pambula. In 1885 John Curtin (future Prime Minister) was born in Creswick, Victoria. They were young men in 1916 when the party split. They endured that tragedy amid the wider tragedy of a generation of Australians meeting death in the Dardanelles, on the Western Front and in the deserts of Palestine. McKell and Curtin were part of a generation of Labor men of exceptional ability. They were entering the prime of their careers when the Great Depression smashed Labor governments across Australia. They witnessed a wasted decade for the party. They had to answer a question that determined the course of their public lives: was Labor ungovernable? Could a party representing the interests of working men and women be regularly elected and re-elected? Was it possible for Labor in government to reconcile the irreconcilable? Could Labor in Parliament and Labor in Conference work through their differences and retain the support of the electorate while being true to the principles which brought Labor into existence?

Men of goodwill surveyed a grim prospect. By the 1930s, Labor in New South Wales had not been able to serve out a second term since its formation. Federal Labor had been elected just once since 1916; that one period of government had resulted in a split three ways inside two years before defeat on the floor of the House of Representatives, an early election and federal Labor's greatest ever defeat.

Curtin became federal leader in 1935 (by one vote). The party was a long way from power, a long way from being competitive. Curtin had to confront directly the condition of NSW Labor, try to prise it from the grip of a demagogue and scoundrel. Without a handsome majority of seats in New South Wales, federal Labor could not win a national election – an iron law of Australian politics. Curtin identified with the devoted minority in New South Wales who had risked all by opposing Lang and Langism. When it became obvious, even to Langites, that the party could not win an election with Lang, efforts to reunite NSW Labor resulted in a Unity Conference and a spill in the state parliamentary leadership. In 1939, Bill McKell became parliamentary leader. He devoted his leadership to fashioning policies that appealed to the middle ground of the New South Wales electorate while never shying from express support for organised labour.

In 1941, John Curtin accepted a commission to serve as Prime Minister after the conservative forces had proved incapable of governing. His government was both one of national unity and expressly Australian Labor. Curtin had come to realise that this World War was very different to the previous; the threat to Australia was present and immediate. The country's defence required the conscription of all available manpower. Curtin was going to compel the enlistment of young men in Australia's armed forces, a course which he had fought against with tenacity in that earlier war. He was confronting demons enough without taking an action that might split his party.

Curtin had deduced that support from the other side of politics in the name of national unity was not worth the candle. Not if the price was Labor tearing itself apart because of the unreasonable sacrifices Labor members and supporters had to make in order to sustain Labor in government. Curtin did not employ the dodge that the parliamentary leadership was attuned to the electorate; Curtin did not quote the popular will against the sensitivities of his party membership. He refused to claim a mandate from the people to justify outrage to Labor sentiment. He remembered too well his youthful self. He would not be oblivious to the rights of his opponents and their inalienable right to oppose him. On the contrary, Curtin was wracked with doubts not about the correctness of his course; no, he questioned his right even to make a decision that he had denied was the right of authority to make in that earlier war. Facing his demons, overcoming doubts about his fitness to decide, Curtin knew that ignoring opposition from within the Labor Party was the route to schism. Persuading a majority within the Labor Party of the rightness of his cause was the means by which Curtin intended to proceed. No other course availed itself to this Labor man.

Curtin devoted his remaining years to the prosecution of the war, which necessarily required expending precious reserves of energy persuading Labor recalcitrants of the wisdom of his course. Curtin relied on the time-honoured processes of Labor governance – decisions made by Labor in Conference, decisions made by Labor in Caucus – to achieve support for conscription. He carried the party with him on each issue. Curtin visited each state executive; he addressed the state trades and labour councils. He spoke to anyone who could influence the decisions of delegates to the ALP Federal

Conference. The barest of majorities – four state branches out of six – voted for conscription. Curtin's efforts at persuasion, and his respect for dissent, ensured the ranks of the defeated accepted the decisions of the majority and remained loyal to the wider cause. For keeping the ALP united while leading his country in war, Curtin is properly regarded as Labor's greatest leader.

The McKell model

In New South Wales, all of a decade was required to remove Lang from the Labor leadership and bring his followers back into the fold. The electorate dictated the need for the Labor Party to act. The landslide defeat of 1932 was confirmed in 1935. The failure to recover lost ground in 1938 convinced all but diehards that Labor under Lang was unelectable. Unions and the Labor Council shifted. Curtin was determined to employ all available federal authority to force Lang out. In 1939 a Unity Conference broke the power of the Lang machine. The power to elect the state leader was returned to the state Caucus where it has remained (at least in formal terms) ever since. Without the power to intimidate, Lang had to face a ballot. It was not the rout that good sense might have dictated. McKell polled 13, Lang 12, Heffron 7. All the Heffron preferences went to McKell. In that moment the modern Labor Party in New South Wales was born.

In 1941 McKell led NSW Labor back into government. Labor reclaimed a swag of rural electorates. In government it showed it could be economically responsible. Labor remained united as, with the outbreak of war, expectations necessarily changed. In great part this was due to McKell and the balanced model of Labor governance he developed. It was based on four broad principles:

1 Managing the ALP *and* governing the state are not separate but indistinguishable responsibilities of equal importance.
2 A NSW Labor government must be able to get on with the business of governing unfettered by external direction, especially by trade unions.

3   Labor governments remain answerable to the party, but the machine leadership ensures that Labor governments, after consultation and the satisfaction of honour, achieve an honourable compromise where there are difficulties with Labor's broad constituency. Astuteness all round ensures that Labor governments avoid appearing high and mighty. At the same time the party and its machinery keep their place, mainly out of sight.

4   Consultation, common sense, mutual respect, give and take, something for everyone: these have been the qualities that have characterised NSW Labor governments and their relations with the party.

Such principles are vested with contradictions. The success of the model has depended on astuteness and self-denial. Success in the long term was made possible by acknowledging that affiliated unions remained in control of the annual conference, and that conference would retain its supremacy so long as supremacy was not exercised against a Labor government. There were exceptions over the decades: the conference supported the uniform tax arrangements in the 1940s opposed by McKell; conference insisted on a referendum to abolish the Legislative Council against the wishes of the Cahill government. Correspondingly, the elected government and members of parliament were entitled to insist upon their obligations to deliver good government and took such action as ensured re-election. As a corollary, a Labor government was obliged to expend as much time as was required – beyond inordinate in the view of many subsequent premiers – persuading unions and the wider movement of the merits of the government's programs and the responses forced upon government by unforeseen circumstance. The McKell model demands the parliamentary leadership make every imaginable effort to cosset party opinion, communicate widely, stroke the machine, pay homage to the supremacy of conference at conference itself and at every set-piece occasion where homage might be made. Labor governments would always be doing plenty in many areas so as to convince the party that the government was basically worth the goods.

The parliamentary party is an entity in and of itself. The leader (especially if premier) is part of the decision-making on machinery matters affecting the electoral performance of the party. The machine will back the government on decisions made in Cabinet, including the backing of Cabinet against Caucus. The government will acquiesce in control of the party by unions, so long as unions delivered what the government wanted – including what was not in the interests of union members. The practical working out of this incompatibility relied upon a common-sense awareness that everyone was on the same side: the consequences of electoral defeat were too horrible to contemplate, so together you worked out a way forward that everyone could live with. Somehow, amid occasional outbursts of name-calling in public, the people in disagreement always worked it through.

The McKell model was so successful that Labor in 1944 achieved a huge landslide, the first time a NSW Labor government was re-elected in a landslide. Labor won again, and again, and again. Having not previously been re-elected once, NSW Labor was re-elected seven times. The McKell model delivered government in eight elections over 24 years from 1941 to 1965. It was the same model that Neville Wran followed through another 12 years of government from 1976. McKell remained the paragon for Bob Carr when he returned Labor to power in 1995. The model prevailed for his 10 years in the job. Even as the unions declined and Labor branches faded into pale shadows of what once they had been, respect for Labor's governance – the supremacy of conference, the binding nature of platform and policy – was unchallenged. Why would anyone challenge a model that had served the party so well for so long?

Under the broad parameters of the McKell model, NSW Labor chose its leaders for nearly seven decades. Changing leaders reflected an honourable means of conferring ultimate authority on the pre-eminent person in the ranks of the parliamentary party. Once the decision was made by a majority, the person chosen enjoyed the support of all. A new leader enjoyed considerable goodwill, a goodwill which could remain for the entire period of his leadership if he delivered election victories and treated the party with respect. Sound politics required the recognition of shortcomings and failure. Those were matters to be handled without a public dimension, preferably acknowledged only when the leadership was changing. How NSW Labor changed its leaders after 1939 is an impressive part of its story, a key reason for its dominance of New South Wales politics.

McGirr and Cahill

McKell led Labor until his appointment as governor-general in 1947. A remarkable man McKell: he created the model for modern ALP governance and laid down the broad principles of how an Australian should behave as governor-general. McKell did not, however, secure the succession for the man he wanted. The man most likely to succeed him was Bob Heffron, a veteran of the Lang wars, favoured by the outgoing Premier, his Cabinet colleagues and the ALP machine. Three months before the state election had to be called, Caucus had other ideas. It took four ballots before a majority was reached. James McGirr, a pharmacist from Parkes, won by two votes. In the time remaining – these days regarded as no time at all – McGirr was able to win the election comfortably.

They were not easy years for Labor. The Chifley government lost office, anti-communism was a weapon being deployed against the ALP in all spheres, the forces that would split the party in 1955–57 were well advanced. In 1950 the Central Executive disendorsed four MPs against the advice and pleading of McGirr. Another four MPs lost preselection ballots. In a close outcome, Labor depended for a majority on those the party had set aside. It was fortunate McGirr had fought for their interests. Labor continued in power.

In 1952, owing to ill-health, McGirr resigned. Heffron calculated that the times had passed him by. He did not contest the ballot against Joe Cahill, clearly the coming man. Clarrie Martin, attorney-general for what remains a record term, made the leadership a contest. Cahill won 32 to 14. His leadership was then unchallenged and unchallengeable. His astuteness kept the Caucus out of the frontline of the ALP Split, even as Labor governments fell in Victoria and Queensland. Cahill was aided and abetted by a Catholic hierarchy in New South Wales more worldly-wise than that in most of Australia. He stroked the machine and Annual Conference. To prevail against sceptics in Cabinet and Caucus, Cahill took his vision for an opera house on the harbour foreshore directly to conference.

Then, in 1959, Joe Cahill died very suddenly, the day after leaving a Caucus meeting because he was feeling poorly. The Parliament was in session when the word arrived that the Premier had passed from their midst. He was only 68, just three months older than the party he had led. No one had given thought to the succession, the 'Old Smoothie' was thought to have years ahead of him. In these circumstances, with no time to rally numbers, the machine distant to unfolding events and no cause to delay, the Caucus turned to Bob Heffron, the safest of hands, to confer on him the prize he had been seeking for three decades. Heffron was already one year older than the departed. He may not have made many friends as the years passed but he had run out of enemies. He had been Minister for Education for 15 years by then, a record that will never be beaten. Heffron held Education and the premiership for another year, another feat that no one else has ever attempted.

Years in Opposition: Renshaw and Hills

When Heffron resigned in 1964, having secured a huge win in 1962 off the back of Menzies' credit squeeze, Jack Renshaw was elected as leader unopposed. Each of McKell's successors had been in the Parliament in 1941; they had an intimate knowledge of what Langism had meant to Labor's electoral prospects; they had been witnesses to McKell's sense of the long term, the importance of patience and timing.

Time's fleeting chariot had arrived for NSW Labor. It is not so much that governments have a fixed term or a natural end. It is more that time undermines the capacity of the electorate to be forgiving of shortcomings. The shortcomings mount. An Opposition will get its act together, the prospect of unending wilderness causes the disparate elements to unite behind a leader who is showing signs of credibility. Governments run the risk of not renewing. Newcomers assume that being in government is in the scheme of things – having never tasted Opposition – their egos adjust to the pleasures of power. Arrogance sets in.

Renshaw was wedded to fiscal rectitude at a time when hefty spending was more appropriate, especially on railways and health. State aid to private schools had re-emerged as a defining issue in electoral politics. Renshaw was disposed to begin the long march to taxpayer assistance to non-government schools, especially as Catholics in good numbers were supporting NSW Labor. Menzies had overcome his own prejudices in 1963 to offer grants for science blocks in non-government schools and won an election in part because of that measure. The mid-1960s represent the final haemorrhaging of the Catholic vote for Labor. The ALP Federal Executive overruled a modest measure of state aid. The Liberal leader, Bob Askin, was promising change, moderate reform, concentrated action to get New South Wales moving again.

Labor lost in 1965 ever so narrowly. When the last votes were counted, the last seat decided, more than 12 days had passed since polling day. Becoming accustomed to Opposition was not easy for Labor. Renshaw was unopposed as leader. The coming man was Patrick Darcy Hills, very young by the standards of the government that had fallen. Hills possessed patience. Under no circumstances would he have challenged Renshaw. The narrowness of the result convinced many that the tide would turn readily enough back to Labor. Askin settled into the job all too well. He was a moderate in matters economic – reflective of a boy from Glebe who had an understanding of Labor values. On social issues he was a reactionary. After an electoral redistribution favourable for the government, Labor in 1968 copped the shellacking intended in 1965. Only then, at the bottom of a landslide, did the smarties start to contemplate that Labor could be a generation out of office.

Renshaw did face a challenge after this second defeat. Harry Jensen, a former Lord Mayor of Sydney renowned for his ability to capture media attention, had not made the switch to Parliament all that well. Not from the Left himself – in an era when that term meant something – Jensen allowed his name to go forward against Renshaw. Hills treated the ballot as a proxy for his own bid, which would come soon enough. Renshaw won comfortably but, only months later, he resigned, professing ill-health. Jensen declined a second defeat. The Left ran Jack Mannix, certainly no Leftist, because he was tough and able, perhaps the person who had Askin's measure – assuming that anyone in the ranks of Caucus had that measure. (Mannix warrants more than a footnote in ALP history. He was the earliest and most important political mentor of Michael Egan following the death of Michael's father.)

Hills won the leadership comfortably. In 1971 Labor polled very well, a primary vote in losing that was far higher than Bob Carr managed in three victories. The electoral boundaries – drawn expressly so as to over-represent the country and with several tweaks to maximise the Liberal Party vote – sank Hills. His misfortune was to lead at the same time as Askin, far and away the most capable conservative leader in New South Wales in the past half century. Hills' parallel misfortune was to be leading state Labor at the same time that the Whitlam government used up all the optimism the Australian people were prepared to expend.

Neville Wran and the myth of a Right fix

In 1973 Askin went early. The Queen had just opened the Opera House. Inflation had taken off. Askin ran hard, fists clenched, against federal Labor – 'Keep NSW in strong hands'. No one in the machine gave Hills the ghost of a chance. For some little time they had been preparing to upset the apple cart that had produced leaders for 32 years. Caucus was going to require an infusion of the unknown to address the huge gulf that separated it from recapturing government.

Neville Wran had been at Fort Street Boys' High when McKell was showing what Labor could do. He was at university when McGirr demonstrated how a government could consolidate. He was a barrister with a big future when Cahill took the government to new heights. By 1970, Wran was in the Legislative Council. Within a year he was the obvious alternative to Hills. He needed to change Houses. The 1973 election provided that opportunity.

The events of 1973 warrant close examination, as it was the only successful party-room challenge to a leader between 1939 and the spill of 2009. Under Caucus rules, the leadership falls vacant automatically after each general election or whenever a leader resigns. The record is unique for any party in Australian politics since the achievement of responsible government in 1856. Often do the NSW Liberals spill their leaders.

The great myth is that the NSW Right machine executed the plot that enabled Wran to win against all odds. The truth is otherwise. The atmospherics for change fell into place as people across the factions concluded Hills could not win an election. If Hills lost in 1973–74, he would have lost twice. Two losses were surely tolerance enough. The Left did not have any time for Hills. The Right was preparing those it could influence with word that Hills would have to stand aside. By the standards of today, the undermining was a gentle affair, with only the occasional public dimension. Party polling revealed Hills was a negative. The General Secretary handed the research to Hills, who quietly sent the research to six fathoms. Polling, public or private, was rare and expensive well into the 1970s. Poor polling, as a weapon of calculated aggression designed to demolish a leader's self-confidence, was still in the future. There were also then still rules of war in the Labor Party which made unconscionable a public assault on the elected leader. By 1973, 32 years since McKell had redefined the leader's role, a leader was to be respected, however badly he might be faltering.

Wran needed to bring on-side Jack Ferguson, an MP since 1959, a true believing socialist who had made his own way out of poverty thanks to government training programs and his union. The trust that resulted would be the bedrock of Wran's leadership. Doubt became respect, respect became absolute trust, friendship became an immense mutual affection that only Ferguson's death brought to an end. Two blokes agreeing on an outcome do not make that outcome happen. There was a lot of mechanics ahead.

Wran was in the wrong House and lived in the wrong part of Sydney. He needed a safe seat. Before that, he needed to be able to resign from the Legislative Council without triggering a vacancy that would fall to the Liberals. Under the then Constitution of New South Wales – before the Legislative Council was popularly elected – new MPs were elected by a college consisting of all the Members of the Legislative Assembly and all the sitting Members of the Legislative Council. Effectively a single vacancy in the upper house was decided by a ballot of both houses. At the time this meant a single vacancy would fall to the Liberals and the Country Party who commanded a healthy majority in both houses. On the other hand, two seats simultaneously vacant meant a common ballot by proportional representation: one of the seats would be certain for Labor. Sacrificing a Labor seat would have been unacceptable to Caucus and would have killed Wran's credibility. Step in, Lionel Murphy, federal Attorney-General.

Murphy offered an appointment to the Federal Court to a Liberal MLC, eminently qualified, known to be willing to accept. Wran resigned the same day as the Liberal so as to guarantee the double vacancy. The safe seat was Bass Hill, in Ferguson's part of the world, overlapping with a young Paul Keating's federal seat. The two factions spoke earnestly to possible contenders that the Labor leadership was coming into play; this was a time to do right by the party. The serving MP delayed the announcement that he was not recontesting until after Askin had announced the election. The Administrative Committee imposed Wran by a vote that would have been unanimous if Hills had not attended and voted against. The locals accepted the imposition with good grace. Those then running the factions had troubled to bring them into their confidence.

In the election campaign, Hills performed far better than anyone had expected. The years 1973 to 1975 proved to be of unremitting disaster for Labor across Australia. Even the Dunstan government in South Australia – thought to be very popular, its Premier charismatic – went to the brink. In Queensland, Labor was reduced to a cricket team. In the Northern Territory it failed to win a single seat. Victoria re-elected its Liberal government handsomely. The Western Australian Labor government fell.

New South Wales was expected to be a generational wipeout. That fate was avoided because the machine insisted on a defensive campaign. All resources were concentrated on holding seats. The strategy was to win in two stages – hold whatever was possible in 1973, after which Askin would retire, then throw everything at winning in 1976 under Wran. Hills resented bitterly the assumption of defeat. He kept that resentment to himself until many years later, when it was a safe topic. His stoicism while one-time allies collaborated with his enemies reflected well on his loyalty to the party. Labor held seats it had no business holding. Bar the redistribution, the Legislative Assembly was almost status quo. Patrick Darcy had done well – perhaps too well if the election was supposed to be a prelude to his execution.

The meeting of the State Parliamentary Labor Party in early December 1973 remains the most dramatic of modern times – until, that is, division took permanent residence after 2007. No one present could recall a passage of time more poignant, futures collective and individual on a knife edge. All of the lobbying came down to a ballot between three men – Hills, Wran and Kevin Stewart (a devout Right-winger, who agreed that Hills had to go, but not for an upstart). The influence of the machine in this final act was limited. They provided comfort for three Right-wing MPs inclined to vote for a change; no harm would result from doing what they thought was best. As it turned out, even one vote delivered was everything.

In all, 44 MPs voted that day. All managed a formal vote. Wran polled 18, Hills 17, Stewart 9. After the distribution of preferences it was Wran 22, Hills 22. The returning officer, primed by Ferguson that the leader on primaries had to be declared the winner, duly declared Wran elected. Ferguson was elected deputy leader with an absolute majority – he had scored one more vote than Wran. The result was accepted of the instant and without protest. Not that day or ever after did Hills squeal about the result. He did not allow an anti-Wran group to form. Copping defeat on the chin and getting on with life reflected immense grace.

The myth of a Right fix in 1973 gave birth to serious evil in 1986. A group of wilful machine operatives cited the 'intervention' of 1973 to justify the elimination of all opponents to an unopposed succession by Barrie Unsworth upon Wran's resignation after 10 years in office. Wran played into their hands by announcing his resignation on the stage of the Sydney Town Hall during Annual Conference. The then General Secretary justified the intervention by the 'precedent' of 1973. He and the machine were very public, up front and central in the leadership resolution. Head Office and the Labor Council thought it smart to frog-march alternative candidates, whose prospects they had just crushed, out of the darkness underneath the Town Hall stage into the arc lights of television cameras and flash bulbs.

The Right compounded its folly by having a factional pre-Caucus ballot so that only one Right candidate would contest the leadership in Caucus. Peter Anderson stood against Unsworth in circumstances where he knew he would be annihilated. The Right could not see that Anderson or any other contenders would afford Unsworth the legitimacy he was lacking. Anderson was duly annihilated. Unsworth was unopposed in Caucus, an early sign the Left was collapsing. Unsworth was nigh fatally cruelled by the base stupidity of others. Every day thereafter, he was in catch-up. That he recovered Labor's position before the whole show fell totally apart does not excuse the machine identities who gave him a poisoned chalice when the leadership would likely have been his for the taking in a more open Caucus ballot – after which no one could have denied his legitimacy.

In 1988, Labor suffered its worst defeat since the 1930s. In the ashes, when all possible alternatives had lost their seats, Bob Carr was the standout. Carr was going to receive the support of a Left then in its death throes, plus the vast majority of the Right. For Carr, as for the machine, it was imperative that he appeared to prevail because the Caucus accepted him without any external pressure. Carr badly wanted, all but begged for, an opponent. No one else stood – though one explored the prospect, did the numbers and knew his cause was hopeless. Carr entered his leadership with the abundant blessing that there was no impression he had been imposed. Although he went within a whisker of being challenged in later years, he was re-elected as leader unopposed four more times.

When Carr stood down in 2005, the General Secretary, Mark Arbib, had a definite preference for Morris Iemma to lead and a no less definite view that Carl Scully was unelectable. Arbib was not alone in those views. He said nought on the record; his movements were in and out of shadows. The machine did not lay credit to Iemma's triumph. By learning the lessons of history as it happened, those who drove events in 1988 and 2005 avoided the disaster of 1986. The disaster of 1986 was the result of believing in a myth of your own making.

Chapter 2
Death below

In 2003, under the leadership of Simon Crean, National Conference reduced the proportion of union delegates at future state and national conferences from 60 to 50 per cent. The impact on the character and control of the ALP was zero. An axiom of organisation is that big blocs versus clusters of smaller groupings will mean the big blocs prevail. In public companies, if the largest holding of shares represents 30–40 per cent, that bloc will control the company. So for the ALP, whether the proportion is 60:40, 50:50, 40:60 or 30:70, the ratio amounts to union control of the conference floor. Control of the floor translates into control of the conference agenda, control of proceedings and control of the atmospherics. The group which controls conference will win the positions elected by conference, most importantly the officers of the party, the ruling executive and the delegates to national conference. Control at conference delivers control of the party between conferences and a dominating position at the conference that follows.

At an ALP conference, it is rare that unions vote together as a bloc. They do not have to. Over the years since 1916, they have imposed a culture that is all-pervasive; a culture of pre-meeting

caucuses and caucuses within caucuses; log-rolling to achieve out-
comes; the elevation of loyalty ahead of ability. A spoils culture in
which the purpose of organisation is self-advancement. Unions of
the Right and Left had fought savage battles in earlier decades, but
they had always agreed that unions should control the party. Having
agreed on the fundamental of party organisation when ideologies
divided them, the heirs to the faction labels were scarce likely to
reform the basis of their control when ideology did not divide them.

Arguments in favour of union control require sophistry worthy
of belief in a flat Earth. One argument is that 'unions connect
the party to working Australia'. Odd, then, that over 80 per cent of
Australian workers do not to a union belong. More than 90 per cent
of workers do not belong to unions affiliated to the ALP. Workers
don't belong because they don't want to belong. Contested union
ballots, like attendances at union meetings, reveal how very few
members take the slightest interest in the affairs of their unions.
The proportion of members of affiliated unions who belong to the
ALP is fewer than 0.5 per cent. Belonging to the ALP is not a part
of the life of a modern Australian worker.

Work and union membership once provided a parallel world
of benevolence, in the decades before there was a welfare state –
funeral funds, workers' credit, cooperative retail stores, benefits for
widows and their children, modest measures of relief for unemployed workers in distress, schools of arts and mechanics institutes
with lending libraries and trades courses. The likes of Myer do
not now field choirs and sporting teams. The railway workshops at
Chullora are no longer a rich subculture of theatre and concerts,
bands and sporting teams, excursions beyond work, a first point of
reference for wives and children. The recreation areas at government bus depots are essentially deserted because the staff prefer
to go home between shifts; they own their own cars. The culture
of unions in the workplace has been dead and gone from most of
Australia for 40 years.

The success of the party created by the unions was ultimately
the undoing of the creators. As the often Labor-governed state

mandated technical colleges to provide trades and other courses paid for by tax dollars, the schools of arts ceased to have a purpose. Municipal libraries replaced their lending functions. State pensions began to look after widows, the aged and the unemployed. State banks provided competition for the banks of capital. Once, the ranks of unionists could fill the streets of our towns or cities on days set aside for a demonstration of solidarity. Even in Bowral in the year of Don Bradman's birth, the ranks of workers on May Day filled the main street from side to side and for its length. Now May Day, Labor Day and the union picnic days are no more. The para-world of unions was an anachronism by the 1970s.

The industrial reform program of the Hawke government killed off the vestiges of a union culture in the workplace. Bob Hawke was utterly determined to alter the very conception of Labor in government. Opening the economy to the world had to mean the eventual destruction of union power as he, a former President of the ACTU, well knew. The regulated labour market, hard-won award conditions, centralised bargaining – none of these was going to sur-vive the absence of tariff barriers, the abandonment of a fixed rate of exchange and the end of monopoly status for public utilities. The massive policy shift with all of its cultural portents was not, however, matched by any corresponding shift in the formal gover-nance of the ALP. The party failed to address the anachronism that unions without a social base remained in control of the ALP. While ever the officials of the unions delivered exactly what the federal parliamentary leadership wanted, the unrepresentative nature of the ALP was an asset to Labor in government, not a hindrance. Electoral success was the elixir that sustained the denial of internal party democracy.

The votes of workers in productive employment have always been in play. Employees are not a mass which can deliver govern-ment to Labor, a truth realised at the party's founding by those responsible for taking the message of the embryonic party to vot-ers however those voters might earn a living. Employees align with Labor (if they align with Labor) by slender majorities. Employees with a blue collar (these days a fluoro vest) voted in the majority for the Liberal and National Parties in the federal elections of 1996, 2001 and 2004. Blue collars provided the base vote for One Nation. Throughout the 20th century something less than an overwhelming majority of workers voted ALP.

The great tidal sweep of Australian politics is the clash between personal values and economic self-interest. Labor loses some proportion of the lowly paid when they cease to be lowly paid. It loses them in greater numbers when they relate to non-economic concerns – pornography rampant, standards in schools, crime unpunished, drugs too freely available, a sense that the past was safer, the dangers of globalism, the whole apparatus of uncertainty of which the most palpable is a fear of Australia's borders being unprotected against the arrival of refugees.

Tradespeople and employees on good wages find that they are accumulating a capital surplus which, managed well, leads to investment income, income which is subject to taxation. Do not be around a wage and salary earner when they discover tax is not always an invisible deduction at source. Sportspeople from humble circumstance in receipt of the big payout go Liberal because they hate paying taxes. The number of Test cricketers who have voted Labor is so small as to be notable. Resentment at paying tax has cost Labor voters for much of its history until, under Hawke–Keating, it joined in the auction to cut marginal rates on tax and raise thresholds. That Australia was a low-tax country without sufficient finance for its ongoing services and investment in its public capital was a problem for the future.

Unions lose social relevance

We don't have Labor lawyers any more, big figures around town, big names in the party. More accurately, the solicitors and barristers who service unions are not names around town or the ALP. For generations lawyers with big names – Bert Evatt, Eddie McTiernan, John Kerr, Terry Ludeke, Jack Sweeney, Lionel Murphy, Neville Wran, Jim McClelland, Jeffrey Shaw – were able to lay claim to a political or judicial career (or both) through representing unions in industrial courts and factional battles. Such lawyers are no more. Labor lawyers abound, of course, but they make their reputations in civil liberties, Aboriginal land rights, human rights. Reputations made in those fields do not cut mustard in Labor preselections.

The end of the Cold War meant that the media, other political parties and foreign powers ceased to take an interest in who controls unions. Well into the 1980s, the President of the Commonwealth Conciliation and Arbitration Commission was one of the major figures in Australian public life, at least as big a figure as the Governor of the Reserve Bank. Today the Commission does not exist, the occupant of the equivalent office is unknown to the public.

The collapse of union membership combined with the ending of the Cold War has meant that the great battles for control of unions are in the past. Basic survival has meant that union officials are now well content to run their own patches and to leave once rivals unmolested in control of theirs. Contemporary contests that evoke memories of past viciousness are those involving the interference of one Right-wing union leadership in the affairs of another Right-wing union. Ideology does not separate Left from Right in modern unions. History's prison has determined the label with which union officials clothe themselves. Officials can concentrate on factional affairs to build a position of influence within their faction, easily the best means to place oneself in the queue for a seat in a parliament. That is why taking a job in a union – any union selected at random – is a stepping stone for the ambitious. Previous work experience, if any, is entirely irrelevant.

The ALP has difficulty pretending it is at the centre of a movement when more than nine out of ten Australian voters *cannot* belong to the unions affiliated to the ALP. The leaders of the unions sensibly unaffiliated to the ALP – white collar, education and public service unions for the most part – have no inclination to affiliate and could not carry their membership behind such a venture. The Teachers' Federation was once capable of almost limitless lunacy but successive leaderships have deduced that a union covering servants of the state has nought to gain from formal affiliation with one side of the parliamentary divide.

The non-ALP union leaders understand that affiliating to a political party immediately surrenders operational freedom and a good deal of credibility with that large number of members and potential members who customarily vote Liberal, National or other. The ALP has managed to construct a governance which expressly excludes from any meaningful role all of the following:

- 90 per cent and more of Australian workers
- the only section of trade union membership which is showing any capacity to grow
- Australians who have retired
- Australians who work at home without payment
- the unemployed
- the self-employed
- students
- much of the public service
- all of teaching and education
- most professionals and employees in every industry with potential for dynamic growth.

Those who state (an altogether different verb to 'believe') that unions should control the ALP fall into two categories: (a) fools or (b) those who gain a material benefit from this posture. It is chilling that the rapid diminution in the ranks of category (a) is more than matched by the growth of category (b).

Much of rural and regional Australia is without unions and unionists, except for those in education and public employment. Scarcely a retail store in any country town has a union member. Entire industries, bustling with growth – such as all the mines in the Pilbara – have discouraged union coverage by paying workers more not to belong. Finding the means to counter employers who make it materially attractive not to belong to a union has defeated modern unions. Employers are prepared to pay above industry standards in order to achieve an absence of any form of union oversight in their workplaces.

The chemistry of ALP organisation

Factions are the unavoidable consequence for an organisation in which there is a democratic and competitive struggle for power. In a political party, the struggle over policy and ideology expresses itself in many forms, most kinetically by way of the battle over text and emphasis and priority. The struggle is resolved by way of the election and appointment of the personnel inside and outside Parliament who are the custodians of the text. The ministers in a Labor government control the mechanisms to turn text into law and action. Rhetoric about mobilising the masses, direct action, using industrial might – all have passed from the lexicon of Labor. Local government is small beer. Capturing parliaments with a view to placing Labor in government is what matters. From legislation, from the levers available to an executive government, power flows.

In any human grouping much above two, alliances will form: people have ideas in common, interests in common. Ambitions overlapping cause individuals to coalesce. Not everyone can win everything, not everything is on offer at once. Those who endure have a chance of winning a prize. Supporting winners stores capital. Supporting losers stores capital. Just as surely, participation in a contest builds enmities and resentments from those not supported.

Alliances may be shifting; they may exist for a single purpose. When alliances are settled and become a part of the institutional arrangements of the party, more formalised factions become a part of the landscape. The existence of factions is neither good nor bad, only their effect – which is a judgement that will tend to reflect whether the observer is a beneficiary or a victim of a factional play.

Factions in the ALP operate in public, at least since the 1980s. John Ducker, the NSW Right's strongman through the 1970s, would look down the lens of a television camera and deny there was a Right inside the ALP. One of the first acts of Paul Keating as President of NSW Labor was to proclaim the existence of a Right faction – under the amusing name of Centre Unity – which would operate openly. Generally, factions are the party's least attractive feature. Being unattractive is not intrinsic: factions can agree to promote talent (as a Troika of three wise men did in South Australia for decades); they can be covert (as all factions tried to be until the 1980s); they can be the source of strength and encouragement, as they were to John Curtin as he battled alcoholism after he had lost his seat in 1931; they can be seen as positive, as was the case as recently as 1983 when the factional leaders in the federal ALP Caucus agreed to promote the most able to be ministers, not themselves – a situation fairly well forfeit by 1987 and utterly absent by the time Caucus ceded the selection of ministers to the leader's prerogative in 2007.

The challenge for the founders of an organisation is regulating competition for control of the organisation in an unknown future when the founders will no longer be present. Struggle for control of the organisation is what causes the depth of conflict that can result in schism and split. For periods during and after the two World Wars, ideology entered the equation when one vision of a workers' utopia caused men and women to fight unto political death for the soul of the Labor Party. With the ending of the Cold War, the factional system has lost its connection with ideology or the realm of ideas. Ideology has passed from the factional firmament.

The factional system since the end of the Cold War turns on the regulation of conflict. The leaders can and will bury their differences beyond public gaze – not a hard task since nothing much divides them except arguments over the appropriate division of paying jobs. The modern factional system is built on a culture of mutual dislike leavened by calculated cooperation. This is most obviously the case inside the parliamentary parties. Now that the separate factions have a quota of positions, either by formalised rules on proportional representation or by binding deals, competition arises *within* the factions for the spoils available. Competitors are notional allies. The frustrations of ambition thwarted are directed inwards to fellow members of the faction. An inward direction of competition to intra-factional discourse has occurred because the factions are formal identities with their own officials and fixed dates and times for meetings. When factions were less formal, they did not meet as standing bodies which asserted the right to anoint candidates and bind supporters. Once upon a time, Caucus elections were all-in scrambles in which anyone could nominate, factions did not presume to approve candidates or endorse them. Votes were cast in secrecy. A factional caucus now meets and endorses candidates beforehand. In the absence of secrecy, each vote is checked by factional overseers before being placed in the box. The exercise eliminates any prospect of independence.

Death of an ALP Left

Once the Labor Party stopped believing in socialism as an achievable reality, those who described themselves as Left inside the ALP had no end of a problem. In the time-honoured fashion of politics, they solved the dilemma of what remained for them by ignoring the question. All those Labor MPs who wore the label Left – which came with the inconvenience of 'socialist' in the faction's title – still found cause to remain members of the ALP. They have not been required to explain why they are living inside a phantasmagoria.

You cannot be a Left-winger unless you believe in socialism. Minus socialist beliefs, being on the Left is a lifestyle choice, a label vested in heroic non-meaning like being a Jacobite after Culloden when the Stuart cause was lost for all time. Those who have benefited from wearing the label have offered wobbly definitions of what being Left means to them. The more sensible do not even bother. Socialism was a relic of whatever meaning, if any, to suit an inconvenience. The ALP settled the meaning for itself in 1922 when it defined its broader objective as support for the socialisation of the means of production, distribution and exchange. In the context of a parliamentary democracy, for Labor in government until the late 1980s, socialism used to mean at least the following:

- public ownership
- progressive taxation

- redistribution of wealth
- redistribution of opportunity.

If you do not tick those boxes – not a big ask – you are not a socialist. When Labor governments act antipathetically to these tenets and not one minister or MP resists that course (other than rhetorically), one is entitled to draw the conclusion that the attachment of those labelled 'Left' to socialism is lip service. No force describable as a 'Left' has engaged in active contest within the ALP over ideas, policies or a framework to respond to unfolding issues, since the mid-1980s.

On objective criteria, Robert Gordon Menzies was well to the left of any minister in contemporary Labor governments. Menzies believed in high rates of tax for high income earners, pump-priming the economy, public ownership of telephones, airlines and banks, centralised wage fixing, legislated protection of union rights and the right to bargain collectively.

The broad discourse of Australian politics from 1941 to 1983 was inside a Leftist prism. Since 1983, the free market has reigned. The Left used to believe in building Jerusalem. Through the vehicle of the Australian Labor Party and the forms of Australian democracy, the Left aspired to employ the power of the state to transform society by eliminating disproportionate private wealth. The Labor Left believed that the rule of law and the will of the people could achieve that objective through legislation, regulation and public administration. The dispossessed would be assisted by the diversion of tax revenues and public services to reach the heights of their ability.

To be on the Left meant being committed to the social reconstruction of our society. Being on the Left is not a matter of touching the buttons that result in a warm inner glow. Being Left is not a matter of supporting the underdog or being good and virtuous. There is nothing exclusively Left about being humanitarian.

It is not about supporting the entry of refugees – which places you beside an ALP Right-winger like John Robertson, a Liberal MP like Petro Georgiou or Cardinal George Pell. Being humanitarian might mean you are a Christian or Jew or Muslim or a Hindu or a non-believing famine relief worker as much as being Left. Mother Teresa believed in combating poverty and starvation. No one called her Left.

Being anti-racist places you with much of decent humanity – alongside Liberal MPs and Malcolm Fraser. Being for Aboriginal self-determination places you with Tories like Billy Wentworth and Charles Perkins. Being for a republic places you with Malcolm Turnbull and the big end of town. Being a militant in industrial affairs places you with doctors and pilots and unions not affiliated to the ALP.

In the absence of an ideology, gesture politics has become all important to those wearing the label of 'Left'. (Hereafter inverted commas will explain that the 'Left' operates in a post-Left reality, excepting those occasions when there is a reference to the Left of history.) Gesture and symbols matter most obviously to the contemporary 'Left' on such questions as the republic, the apology, a bill of rights, none of which distinguish a 'Left' from the ALP Right or non-Labor. The politics of being anti-uranium encapsulated the emptiness of gesture. It is a burlesque worth reciting.

The ALP's internal divisions on uranium mining in the 1980s resulted in the so-called three mines policy. That is, the National Conference expressly authorised the mining and export of uranium from three of the world's largest uranium mines. The Conference stopped at three in 1984 for the sound reason that the output from these three was more than sufficient to meet world demand. In any other country, supporting output of such magnitude would be regarded as rabidly pro-uranium. Not for the 'Left'. Mining and exporting uranium was a scale of wickedness to bring into peril the future of humankind and all forms of life on the planet – unless the uranium was mined from one of the three Australian mines expressly authorised by an ALP National Conference. Preventing the number of authorised mines expanding beyond three duly became a struggle for life and death every inch as momentous as the campaign to preserve humankind from any uranium mining had once been.

It was always understood that the restriction would be lifted as and when the world demand for uranium exceeded output from the three. By this century that time had arrived. In the meantime, the continuing exploration by Western Mining Corporation of Roxby Downs kept adding colossal amounts of ore to known reserves. That extra ore was fine; finding new ore anywhere else was not fine. When BHP Billiton took over Western Mining, its new assay of Roxby added not less than 10 per cent to the known reserves, a quantum greater than the ore that would become available in the next seven mines to come on-line. Reflect on that arithmetic.

To the credit of Kim Beazley he decided to end the nonsense of the three mines policy. Uranium had been the perfect issue for what the 'Left' had become. Unlike the 1970s and 1980s, when a half-million people had marched the streets of Australia's capital cities to oppose uranium mining, by 2007 there wasn't even a campaign of letters to the editor. The National Conference set aside some time, the rhetoric flowed, the outcome was not in doubt. Some wags on the Right thought of switching a bloc so as to embarrass the 'Left' into countering with its own switch. The Conference voted to authorise extended mining. Mining proceeded, the human race survived. We have not heard a word from the 'Left' about uranium in the time since. There is no move to recommit the decision which, one recalls, was about the future of humankind. Are people fooled by this burlesque?

Socialism was buried across the West, then the East, by a prolonged prosperity. The Berlin Wall came down, the Soviet Union collapsed, the former satellites embraced the market and forms of democracy. China has managed to blend a market economy with tyranny. By 2010, when scarcely a blue-collar union is led by a worker who comes from the ranks, those who engage in competition for the ALP's soul fall into the categories of the very comfortable, the rich or the seriously rich. When the conference assembles, there are more millionaires on the floor than there are industrial workers. The few workers from humble circumstance who get elected as conference delegates come from the electorate councils. Union delegations are mainly officials and ring-ins from the political class.

ALP membership has changed to reflect changes in the nature of work. Electoral support for the party has shifted in both directions as people on wages have acquired ownership of their own homes and accumulated other assets. Occupational superannuation was a signal by Labor, political and industrial, that society was moving back to a pre-1945 pre-welfare state equation: prudential action by each individual worker was going to be necessary to replace, certainly to supplement, the pensions other Labor governments had introduced.

The parliamentary parties shifted their policy emphases and forced those changes on the party. The driving force for the economic reforms of the Hawke–Keating era came from the Prime Minister and his Treasurer, who were supported by the leading officials of Treasury and Finance and the inner group of Cabinet rationalists. This leadership group dominated intellectually, they imposed their will on Cabinet, then Caucus, then National Conference. They did not sustain a single defeat along the way. The factions played catch up or were rendered irrelevant.

The Left was traumatised during this process because Gerry Hand and Brian Howe, ministers in the Hawke government, saw no point in poorly argued resistance. They preferred relevance. The Howe–Hand strategy prevailed after 1987, with fateful consequences for the last semblance of unity within what had become a label only.

In Labor's heartland in Australia and equivalent spaces across the democratic world, workers vocalised their resentment at paying taxes. Tories pandered to this disposition, promised to slash said taxes, and struck electoral gold. Competition for cutting taxes replaced the competition for building a better nation. Labor was not uncomfortable in offering rhetoric that amounted to declaring the market to be sovereign and endorsing the notion that citizens are better placed to make their own decisions about how they spend their income.

When the great crisis of capitalism did arrive during 2007–08, Wall Street itself became endangered. The governments of the West nationalised banks and insurance companies. Lines of taxpayer-funded credit were all that kept some of the great corporations in business. The US government became the world's largest home-owner and blithely took ownership of the world's largest insurance company. Wiping out Australia's manufacturing base was fine, sending to the sword jobs and industries in the Illawarra and the Hunter was fine – hurting Manhattan's financial districts was another matter. These might have been times when a real Left could be calling out 'I told you so'. There were no such cries because no one left in the 'Left' had been saying so.

In the 1980s, the Left was utterly routed in the battle of ideas. Post-1989 the 'Left' did not offer a contest. The problem for those MPs and party officials wearing the label was that they were formally committed to a set of beliefs in which either (1) they did not believe a word or (2) they were not going to put their careers at risk by stating what they believed in. Which amounted to the same thing. Not one of the petals put their careers on the line as the Hawke and Keating governments and various state Labor governments sold public assets, corporatised whatever they could, outsourced the delivery of public services and proclaimed the virtues of fiscal discipline.

One understands the dilemma facing beached whales as they look backwards at an ocean they can not re-enter and inland to an unknown environment where they would struggle to survive. Adaptation required pretence and bluster. One is not critical of them for choosing survival. The absence of distinctive ideas did not trouble the inhabitants. The 'Left' bespoke a beliefs system which no longer existed. Wearing that label in public whenever it was convenient conferred seats in parliaments, places in ministries, jobs on staffs, salaries, superannuation units, a place in the sun, relevance inside a Labor Party totally dominated by conservatives who were delighted to be rid of a faction that occasionally troubled itself and the party with pangs of conscience. The salaried element of the 'Left' was by then a huge proportion of its dwindling army – a proportion that was going to become much bigger. These people had obligations to partners, children, mortgages and their own place in the sun. For castaways in a hostile environment, calling themselves 'Left' made eminently good sense.

The 'Left' survives because the ALP relies on factions to make its machinery work. The Right requires an opposition to provide legitimacy for the imposition of its will. The 'Left' has received a leave pass from the Right: never ever would the Right assail the 'Left' for not believing a word of the old stuff. Unlike the era when the Cold War was in earnest, the Right does not use ballots at annual conferences to try to wipe out the 'Left' – even though arithmetically that achievement is within its reach. In a version of cowboys and Indians for adults, one side has taken to smoking cigars on the verandah of the general store.

In the 1980s, as many of the European socialist parties were redefining their objectives and changing their names, the consequence in the ALP of the death of ideas and ideals inside the sputtering Left had the opposite outcome. On the very night that the world beheld the beauty of the people of Germany tearing down the Berlin Wall – the very night – the Steering Committee in New South Wales voted to change its name to 'Socialist Left'. The sponsors of this product relaunch well knew that socialism was dead. When there was a Left in New South Wales with a purpose and a common set of ideals, it did not use that name; when it abandoned any pretence of believing in socialism and opposing the Right, it cloaked itself in a heroic mantle. Acquisition of the heroic name marks the beginning of regulated collaboration with the Right for carving up spoils as they came on offer. The Steering Committee split that night, an outcome traceable to divisions in the parliamentary Left that had their beginnings six years earlier. The divisions became terminal. The faction formally separated into two autonomous groups on that same night in 1989. In due course the faction reunited, though the divisions continued and intensified, becoming sub-tendencies that took on the full apparatus of factions. In due course, the sub-tendencies developed tendencies and institutionalised division. Competition moved ever downwards into ever narrowing necks of bottles: people of well-nigh identical views competed for positions with the result that the most intense hatreds were reserved for people who shared their position in the beliefs spectrum – assuming that beliefs placed factional operatives wherever they found themselves.

The collapse of ideology was matched by abandoning opposition to the direction set by the ruling Right. The place in the sun occupied by the Howe–Hand tendency was so successful a stratagem that the alternative element of the 'Left', being without ideology, proceeded to compete as to which group would be more useful to the Right. This is what the once-proud Left has degenerated into: an all-consuming competition between its groupings as to which can more successfully be incorporated by the Right. Across Australia, in Parliament or the party organisation, there is not one instance of a united Left. Instead, we have a label which is divided into dealing and double-dealing with the dominant Right.

The ALP suffers from the absence of a Left. Without one, there is no opposition to what rapidly becomes the conventional wisdom. Dissent is stilled. In the absence of a Left, a vast territory has been forfeited for the Greens to occupy. In the inner-cities, the Greens are stalking Labor. These adherents include former communists and refugees from the ALP's inner-city wars of the 1980s. They know the language of what used to be the Left, because that is what they are, unchanged, unrevised, unquestioning. The Greens wiped out the ALP in the local government elections in Sydney's inner-city in September 2007. What remains of an ideological left are amorphous groupings of academics and cultural leftists. They are entirely irrelevant to the discourses of the ALP and the decisions of Labor in government.

A grouping calling itself 'Left' has remained in the party even as the core issue of enterprise and infrastructure – the public ownership of the means of production, distribution and exchange – has passed into private ownership. Even as state aid flows to private schools. Even as an independent foreign policy has become pro-American. Even as business interests and property developers have acquired influence through donations to the party which dwarf union contributions.

At the other end of the spectrum, a Catholic-based Right has remained in the party even as Labor governments have legislated for or acquiesced in no-fault divorce, homosexual law reform, the ending of censorship, legal abortion. It is no bar for advancement within the Right, as once it certainly was, to be an adulterer, a philanderer, a divorcee or to express yourself as you want sexually.

The net result is a convergence of views, cooperation for positions, agreement to shut down dissenting voices. The consequences of the absence of a contest is most obvious in the hollow shell which ALP annual conference has become.

Membership collapse

Throughout the past decade, over 100 ALP branches have folded in New South Wales (see Appendix A). One or more branches fold per month most months of a year. Branches are allowed to go under only when inactivity has become unconcealable. A formal branch quorum is an unambitious seven; in country New South Wales the quorum is just five. Many branches are phantoms or paper frauds. Attendance at branch meetings has been sliding for two decades. Those few attending are all that remain of the commitment which the Labor movement used to proclaim.

The raw numbers of membership reveal a similarly shocking state of affairs (see Appendix B). Financial membership of the NSW Branch in 2009 was 15 385 and falling. In order to claim concessions on membership fees, some 60 per cent of members profess to be retired, unemployed or full-time students. Fewer than 7000 members work for a living, a remarkable statement about the so-called 'party of the workers'. Fewer than 1000 play any sort of active role in the party.

Without getting lost in numbers, the ALP across New South Wales has fewer than half the membership it possessed after the Second World War and before the Split of the 1950s. Membership was on a steady rise through the Whitlam era as Labor voters wanted to connect directly with the sense of hope that Gough Whitlam's vision for Australia provided. Following the massive electoral defeats in 1975 and 1996 there were sudden surges of support. Few of those new members stuck around for more than a year. In a study of three branches in the suburbs of Sydney for each year of the 1950s, carried forward into the 1960s and 1970s, this author discovered that 24 per cent of new members did not renew after one year, 70 per cent had disappeared by year five. They had gone whether the local party held the local seat or not, gone whether the branches were fascinating or stultifying, gone however predominant the ALP was electorally. Ordinary Australians wanting to be politically active – and not seeking a material reward – cannot be bothered with an organisation which they have no prospect of influencing in any worthwhile way.

Official reviews of what is wrong with the ALP return to the same nostrums: make meetings more interesting, make meetings more accessible, hold meetings in the day or on weekends, streamline procedures, bring in guest speakers, break into discussion groups. Each and every remedy has been applied by every branch that sought to hold its numbers. None work. The opposite comes to pass. A branch with interesting meetings, blessed with an efficient secretary, trying to make things happen, corresponding with Head Office, corresponding with Labor governments, finds that nothing happens. Replies do not come, replies are tardy, replies are prepared by a computer in response to key words. The better a branch is, the more it seeks to be involved in the wider affairs of the party, the more total is its failure. Members who want a return on the investment of time and energy look elsewhere. Anyone involved in community politics will learn that the ALP offers the poorest return on the investment of their time – unless they crack the jackpot of a seat or a paid position. Remuneration and its prospect have become the overriding reason to join the ALP.

Branches are on life support paid for by the taxpayer. For a branch to get its breath on a mirror all it has to do is meet every three months. Muster seven members (or just five in the country) at the same place at the appointed date and time – and the branch lives. To achieve that assembly, a meeting notice will go forth. The staff of a Labor MP will have prepared that notice. The taxpayer has paid for the paper, the ink, the envelope, the label, the postage and the staff time involved in the despatch. If using tax dollars to mail ALP meeting notices and produce other ALP materials were a criminal offence (as it should be), ALP meeting notices would not be posted. Within a month at the latest 300–500 branches in New South Wales would cease to exist.

The political class

What really separates the factions is competition for jobs. The immediacy of a job is the principal means of recruiting operatives, a practical step backed up by tantalising portrayal of a future with glitter and power. Recruiting troops for an army on the ground used to be undertaken at a local level by a local hopeful seeking support for a local seat. Now recruiting is a centralised industrial process supervised by the leadership of the factions. Newcomers are attracted to the prospect of employment (which may not materialise) and the prospect of a seat somewhere down the track (which is even less likely to materialise). For a young person with political ambitions, deciding whether to join the Labor Party or the Liberal Party is often a matter of who made the more convincing offer.

The party has become professional as the factions have hardened into employment mechanisms. Ministerial staff has grown beyond all imagining. Lloyd George, as the Prime Minister of Britain during and after the Great War, had a staff so large it was referred to at the time as 'the garden suburb'. Lloyd George's staff was less than the number who serve a Premier of New South Wales. Members of the NSW Legislative Assembly did not acquire private staff until

1975. The first of the private ministerial staff, other than press secretaries, were appointed under Whitlam in 1972. The appointees were meant to provide a minister with advice different to that of the public service on matters of public policy, not be taxpayer-funded operatives for party politics.

Factional operatives are members of the only class which has survived into this century – the political class. They are a coherent grouping which fulfil all of the Marxist definitions of class: consciousness of each other, action in concert, action in self-interest. The emergence of a political class in the 1980s, its total conquest of the key mechanisms of the ALP by the 1990s, is best explained through the science of natural selection, a tenet of Darwin's theory of evolution that each species will either adapt to its new environment or will perish.

Preselection for Labor seats was once a possibility for every member of the ALP, usually a local, who had put in the years of spade work as a loyal soldier in the cause. If hard work at a local level were the route into Parliament, then that was the route that generations of the ambitious pursued. Gough Whitlam QC, a barrister with a growing reputation, won his preselection for the safe and sprawling seat of Werriwa by dint of meticulous attention to his local branch members. Famously, he chopped wood for one preselector as he was outlining the reasons for his preferment. Potential candidates held down real jobs, raised families, lived lives that immersed them in local communities. There were no shortcuts, except in marginals in which 'star quality' was occasionally accepted as essential to win the middle ground. The system often came up short, some utter dolts won preselection for safe seats. The same system also produced men of the calibre of Ben Chifley, Bill McKell and Bob Carr, as well as some of the most talented MPs Australian public life has ever seen.

The localised nature of preselections afforded Labor MPs a measure of independence from party machine and parliamentary leadership alike. Provided they served their local party interests, MPs were invulnerable. A critical mass of MPs answerable only to their branches created a parliamentary Caucus with a character of resolute independence. Caucus independence came to an end in New South Wales when Labor Members of the Legislative Council entered the Caucus in mid-1985. MLCs were preselected centrally. To become an MLC, a candidate had to be a liegeman of a faction. If an MLC wanted to retain his or her seat, they had to remain loyal to the faction. A critical mass of MLCs with loyalties to central factional machines entirely altered the culture and power relationships inside the Caucus. Add a critical mass of Members of the Legislative Assembly who were imposed by central preselections, and the result is a contemporary State Parliamentary Labor Party disconnected to historical Labor, disconnected to the ALP below.

The best way to come to the attention of a modern faction is to obtain employment in one of the staff positions in the gift of the factions. The factions have evolved to exercise levels of command over their ranks previously unthinkable. Inside one generation, the catchment for parliamentary preferment is increasingly restricted to those who work on the staff of a minister, the ALP office or an affiliated union. The Liberal Party, slower to adapt, has similarly been showing preferment to its own staffers.

The consequence conforms with the laws of nature. The ALP has been narrowing the gene pool from which MPs might emerge. Life's experiences become limited. After graduation from university (or after dropping out), those aspiring to be MPs reckon their best chance is employment in a union or on the staff of a minister. One can scarcely blame the ambitious for adapting their campaigns for preselection to the changing realities of advancement. The result is an adaptation of life's arc to meet rigid factional expectations about mobility, mating, tribal loyalty, ideological carapace and camouflage.

The political class has captured the Labor Party in parliament and the machine. Their knowledge of Labor history and respect for Labor's traditions is zero; sub-zero really, as contempt for branches and the old ways is a staple of conversation. The Labor Party is a career path, one stage in life. When the parliamentary phase is over, so very often is the Labor Party phase of their lives.

Host body

Unions provided the host body for the take-over of the Australian Labor Party. Changes in the Australian and world economies, technological advances, revolutions in the organisation of work, these changes served to make unions in the private sector somewhere between unimportant and irrelevant. In the 1970s and 1980s, as blue collar unions were no longer able to rely on talent emerging from their ranks, so their benighted, ageing leaderships brought in tertiary-educated young blokes with a stint in the ALP, political operatives who did not come from the ranks of the workforce covered by the union. More likely than not, these operatives had never held nor would ever hold a real job in their lives – 'real' in this case meaning one where the employer would not tolerate the employee working on behalf of the ALP or its interests during work hours. Each time that union officials permitted the ALP factional leaderships to place an operative on their staffs, the existing leaderships acquiesced in a reverse take-over.

As officials who had once worked in the industry retired, they were replaced by younger men, in due course women, from outside those industries. Inside one generation, the placemen of faction became the union leaderships. The political class took control of ALP head offices at the same time. The political class moved toward a monopoly in candidate selection for any winnable seat in the state. The parliamentary parties became the domain of the political class. Right-wing MPs engineered a reverse take-over of the Right faction, though their control of Conference depended still on the union bloc vote. The union bloc vote guaranteed Right MPs in good standing protection against challenge in a preselection, however unworthy or dull those MPs might be.

As union leaderships too fell to the political class, they further disconnected from the workers they were created to represent. Jobs in unions came to depend on the old school tie, the right university, the right department within a university. Marrying smart helped, as did your father and mother and uncles and older brothers. One union might be the alumni of a de la Salle college, another the industrial relations department of an inner-city university. Neither BHP nor CSR at their notorious worst was as nepotistic as unions (and the ALP) have become. Future preferment was becoming more and more dependent on the bed in which you were born and/or the bed you shared.

There was nothing much officials could do about the continuing decline of unions and unionism. Taking over these moribund institutions provided value for one reason and one reason only – with them came a controlling parcel of shares in the ALP that delivered the keys to the kingdom of one side of Australian politics. The situation was apposite to the strategies of the corporate raiders enjoying vogue at that same time. Raiders will go after an ailing manufacturer not for its products, not for its assembly line, certainly not with a vision of turning the show around. The raiders understood the unrealised value of the freehold real estate underlying the factories just waiting to be sold. The ALP affiliation was the asset of value for the new generation of union officials.

Through the 1980s and 1990s, unions amalgamated many times over, a process which divorced them even further from the bonds of loyalty between workplace, calling and unionism. By 2008, the unions affiliated to the ALP were in decline across the board. They enjoyed a fillip owing to an attack by the Howard government when it passed legislation restricting their ability to protect basic wages and conditions under a contract-based system of employment. If the Howard government had legislated in favour of ballots by the membership on such questions as affiliation to a political party and the making of donations to election campaigns, they would have carried the day and completely broken the political power of the unions. The Howard government was never going to act that way: the Liberal Party has an acute understanding of what is the ALP's most unattractive feature.

Qualities like intellectual growth and the faculty for curiosity are dangerous for inhabitants of the political class. People in real jobs, facing the challenges of life's hazards, necessarily change over a lifetime. Some become more conservative, some not. Ideas and values reflect those changes. Not for a political class whose employment is wholly dependent on never stepping outside the prevailing orthodoxy.

Professionalisation of the factional leaderships has reduced the need for a membership below and much else of the party apparatus. Public funding of election campaigns and pandering to the big end of town with high-cost corporate dinners and benefit-related personal fundraising mean the machine can do without traditional sources of funding from unions and branches. The phalanxes of ministerial staff can be and are deployed where required. When the whistle was blown in 1995 by the Liberal–National Opposition on the propensity of the ALP Right-wing machine to warehouse operatives on the staffs of MPs, the whistle was put away of the instant. It did not do for the Opposition to get too particular about the use of staff, postage or stationery. Taxpayer-funded direct mail and saturation advertising have replaced the humble foot soldier delivering pamphlets. Party identification on the ballot paper means that standing outside a polling booth with how-to-votes has been reduced to a show of strength of little practical consequence.

It is very rare for a local area to run its own campaign all on its own. Young people and new members of all ages, the future stalwarts, once learned the basics of campaigning from the old masters who took them around the hustings. Old hands instructed newcomers in pamphlet design, designing and placing newspaper advertisements, lodging material with printers and collecting the finished product. They staffed offices, handled enquiries, met visiting dignitaries, organised meetings and rallies. The most fortunate were able to listen to tales of derring-do from a legendary past when the Labor Party was a crusade, stories imparted by those who had been there five decades or so earlier. Now the ALP grants certificates to those who pass through formal courses on campaign methods.

Building a spaceship

In every other crisis of identity and electoral melancholy, the Labor Party has drawn on history. In adversity the ALP has been magnificent, the most resilient creature on the Australian political landscape. But now? Where exactly does modern Labor draw from? Once upon a time Labor could draw from all the factories in Australia and all the mines, the railways and ships and trucks, the waterfront, the gangs working in the open air. It could supplement that gene pool with a growing army of adherents in the liberal arts, teaching, the law and other professions, essentially anyone characterised as progressive in a whole range of social issues, foreign policy, nationalism, civil liberties. Either directly or through the ranks of union officials, Labor could draw on the best out there for renewal. Each such source of supply has dried up.

The parliamentary leaderships have been forced to supply their own answer – liegemen in the image of themselves and 'stars' recruiting from outside the ranks of the ALP, relying on factional tyranny to impose them as required. The assumption is that celebrities, some with successes in other lives, will adapt to the specialist demands of parliamentary and ministerial office in the absence of the most basic party political experience. Behind that assumption is the notion that the successful graduates of faction, the leaders of the political class – a cabal enjoying a near-monopoly in candidate selection – possess insight superior to what remains of the ALP membership.

The Liberal Party is able to conduct preselections for its safest of seats in Wentworth, Bradfield, Kooyong, Higgins and McPherson, witness blood-curdling contests down to the wire, permit the local memberships to play the major role in the decision, yet emerge from the contests renewed and without the need to hear appeals from the defeated. The Labor Party in New South Wales cannot rely on its membership in safe seats to provide candidates of even fair-to-average quality. A preselection in a vacant safe Labor seat in New South Wales is certain to occasion allegations of dirty tricks, defunct branches suddenly reactivated, material rich in possibility for investigative journalism and police inquiries. The probable winner will be a dud, tainted by what was required to put together a winning vote. At the end of the pain, the prospect of quality emerging is remote in the extreme.

Labor's parliamentary parties recognised that the Labor Party had largely disappeared below. Instead of fostering a revitalisation, as Tony Blair had for a while sought in Britain, instead of reaching out to provide a sense of worth to ordinary Joes and Joannes, the leaderships elected to disconnect the parliamentary parties from the party membership so as to become a spaceship soaring free. Instead of encouraging followers of promise to get involved at the humblest points – as staff members and union officials once were – then support such people in a contest, the leaderships have elected to suspend democracy in favour of imposing liegemen in safe seats where they could not determine the outcome if the decision was one for the local membership. Prior involvement with the ALP was minimal. Often these candidates joined the ALP at the same time as they nominated for selection. The consequence has been an unarrested decline in the membership ranks. A sense of futility has become all pervasive. With preferment dependent on patronage from above, MPs possess a minimal connection to the ALP except as an acquired taste. If the leaderships get selection wrong, addressing those shortcomings of character and ability is not possible by the ancient processes of party democracy. Once inside the parliamentary tent, an incumbent is safe except for offences against the leadership and the faction.

The cultural outlook of a bird of passage is necessarily much different to a stalwart in his or her native habitat. Quota rules about women were the perfect smokescreen to justify smashing localism and participatory democracy. Novices became ministers because their patrons insisted on their selection. Leaders have achieved their wishes by *force majeure*. Parliamentary parties have become self-perpetuating oligarchies. Advancement has come and will continue to come exclusively from looking inwards to the powers that be.

Once it was the case that Labor leaders looked out to draw from those who had nurtured them, guided them, selected them. When you have been imposed, there is no 'out there' out there. You look inwards because those inside the spaceship sponsored your boarding and will, as readily, facilitate your disembarkation. The core skill of the old-time politician was sniffing the wind, a sense of what was right, what could play and a willingness to turn opinion around. Politics was about values. Leadership used to mean adopting unpopular positions because you thought those positions were correct; leadership used to mean confidence in your ability to persuade the electorate of the correctness of the course that you have proposed.

Experience alone confers those skills. In the absence of an apprenticeship on the backbench and, before then, in the branches and councils of the party, ministers and leaders will lack key skills. Once new ministers relied on the permanent heads of the public service and the senior hierarchy whom they had inherited, men and women who had spent their adulthood working for governments of all persuasions. Public servants had known a culture in which offering frank and fearless advice was the norm and ministers listened before deciding. Entirely absent was a sense of apprehension that advice unwelcome to a minister would occasion adverse consequence for a public servant.

The senior ranks of the state public service are just as likely to be populated by former political staffers, the retinue of a previous ministry. (To be fair, some staffers have managed well the transition to professional public servant according to the only judgement that counts – those who work with and for them.) Senior public servants are now following ministers across portfolios. In the absence of disinterested advice, in the absence of personal experience, ministers are highly susceptible to those who base their advice on opinion polling and market research. The advice from such people is a neat package – the problem explained, the solution offered. Once such advisers gain the ears of those who matter, they will acquire guru status. Governments under stress depend ever more on gurus for

the way out. The most able of the gurus have established professional advice companies after their days on staff. Even the politics
and values pursued by Labor governments have been out-sourced.

The contest in 2008 over electricity between the New South Wales
government and the Australian Labor Party was a test of what control the party enjoyed over the spaceship ruling in its name. Those
sitting for the test were the delegates from Right-wing unions and
electorate councils. These people had to choose between their leadership group in government – graduates from the staffs of unions
and ministers – and the leadership of the Right-wing unions, who
themselves aspired to enter a parliament. The conflict could not
have happened under the McKell model.

Chapter 3
The rise of Morris Iemma

Giuseppe and Maria Iemma arrived in Australia in 1960. The young couple, recently married, had departed their village in Calabria, what had been their whole world. Within a year their only child was born – a son, Maurizio, who became known outside the family as Morris. When Morris was six, the family moved from the inner-city to Beverly Hills in Sydney's southern suburbs, where they have lived all the years since. The Iemma parents both worked, a variety of jobs in car building, textiles, print shops. Getting and keeping work was often hard with English language difficulties.

Giuseppe had been a communist in a country which enjoyed the largest Communist Party membership outside the Iron Curtain. He did not abandon his faith in a new country. Both parents valued politics and political discussion. Morris Iemma grew up in a household where politics was the staple of discussion. More than discussion; it was a household which believed in collective action to protect the worker in his or her place of work and believed in the possibility of reform by political action. It was a household in which an emerging Gough Whitlam was the hero. Giuseppe took his son to Whitlam rallies. He kept a close eye on the Labor leader in newspapers. Television and radio delivered the Labor leader into the household. In 1974 the Iemmas took Australian citizenship as a tribute to their hero.

Textile factories were a long way from the front line of Australian politics. For the Iemmas and immigrants like them, the struggle for justice and dignity was renewed daily. The Iemmas were more fortunate than most migrant workers. They had the assistance of an interpreter, counsellor and advocate: that person was their adolescent son. Because he had to, Morris read the documents his parents brought home. He learned early about the importance of phrasing, getting words to express a clear meaning. Morris read the text of industrial awards, he saw how words could define – by limiting or enhancing – entitlements and working conditions of workers who enjoyed no protection beyond those words. He apprehended those words afforded no protection unless there was someone who would argue the intent of those words on behalf of workers. Morris was the family member who rang government departments and the union office. He was developing a great interest in the law and its possibilities. In the media, he saw ACTU officials argue for better conditions for workers and Tories argue against. Which side of politics he would choose was not in doubt. It was no less in doubt that he would choose to be involved in his party when he was old enough to join. His father had always believed in being involved.

Morris Iemma joined the Australian Labor Party in 1977, age 16. For a young man wanting to make a practical contribution, the Communist Party was not an option. The final trigger for someone joining the ALP of their own accord was an encounter in a neighbourhood shopping centre with local branch stalwarts who were standing beside a card table on which a poster was leaning. The poster carried a photo of Neville Wran with local candidates. Morris approached the people at the table. Conversation explained what a branch was, when and where it met. At the next meeting of the Beverly Hills Branch, Morris Iemma applied to join the Labor Party. The meeting was not what he expected. Absent was debate on the great issues of national politics. The first meeting and those which followed were boring to a young man seeking stimulus.

The branch, like much of the Labor Party wherever the party is a significant presence in local government, was mired in the intricacies of the local council. No detail went unspoken at the meetings, as anything up to four local aldermen reported on the council. The branch was moderate, not heavily factional, supportive of the local MPs whose power bases were in the big branches elsewhere. A lot of self-employed people belonged – a reason for the branch's comparative indifference to the wider internal party struggles taking place so near. Far from disillusioned, worldly wise in a hurry, Morris found the local ALP fascinating. How the party worked absorbed his maturing thoughts on the possibilities of action. Iemma applied himself to understanding the structure of the ALP and its rules. He became an expert on machinery matters.

Morris continued with his studies after leaving Narwee Boys' High. He undertook Economics at the University of Sydney, then Law at the University of Technology. He was a natural at branch politics, a recruiter out of the ordinary who was becoming known. His allegiance was to the ALP Right. Although his father was a communist, he was also socially conservative. The position of the Left on family issues and abortion offended Iemma. The Right cultivated him; the Left did not. The side that encourages a coming player is likely to hold him. For a while he worked for the Commonwealth Bank Officers' Association before accepting a job with Senator Graham Richardson after Hawke had returned federal Labor to power. Morris Iemma enjoyed a lot of freedom to advance the cause of the Right in the local area. His recruiting of Lebanese members was affording him a dominating influence in many branches

Moving into Parliament

The 1988 state election had devastated Labor. All three local seats had fallen to the Liberals. In a landscape of little opportunity, Iemma adhered to an ancient principle of politics and life: he made himself available when not many were offering. Beverly Hills Branch was a composite, straddling three seats. Being split three ways usually meant playing the role of an extra in each of the electorate councils, unless someone with energy and ambition built the branch membership across the board: then a composite branch enjoys an influence not available to branches wholly within the one electorate. Iemma possessed that energy.

Iemma sought and won a contested preselection in 1990 for the difficult seat of Georges River. His employer, Graham Richardson, advised him against seeking a proposition so dicey, advice which had no effect on a determined young man. The Liberal Greiner government was riding high, Bob Carr was not cutting through, the commentariat was declaring a walkover for Nick Greiner whenever he might choose to take New South Wales to the polls. A redistribution of electoral boundaries turned possibilities upside down. Georges River was made ultra-safe for the Liberals. Neighbouring Hurstville was definitely winnable, especially when the sitting Liberal MP refused to recontest a seat so changed. Others had claims on Hurstville. The Greiner government had reduced the Legislative Assembly from 109 seats to 99. Sitting MPs on both sides were considering the same turf. ALP Head Office decided to step in and make their own allocations of who scored what. Head Office would choose the winners and losers in search of a balanced factional outcome in a spread of seats that needed resolving from Coogee on the eastern seaboard to a surplus of sitting MPs in the Bankstown area and Parramatta, as well as the difficulties in Sydney's south. Head Office chose Iemma for Hurstville.

The campaign of 1991 was memorable because every commentator wrote off Carr. Not one poll gave him a chance. The mood of the voters was otherwise. Carr crafted a campaign perfect for the circumstance. In a tight election that resulted in a hung Parliament, Iemma romped in – his local campaign was one of technical perfection – but not by such a margin that he thought he could relax. With every marginal seat the subject of ongoing attention by both parties, Iemma was determined not to let the side down by any lack of performance. For three years he campaigned non-stop. He read about the cutting edge of American campaign techniques in journals devoted to their practice. Wherever he could, he applied and adapted his reading. Iemma was attentive to the experiences of other Labor MPs, state and federal. He was forever testing and refining. In 1995, in the election that brought Carr to power, Iemma increased his majority. In Labor circles he was regarded as a campaigner supreme.

His interests remained the same as the young boy who had witnessed the disadvantage encountered by his parents. His ambition was to be the Minister for Housing so that he could pursue policies on public and affordable housing. He was concerned about issues of mental health and disability services. For much of the first term of the Carr government, as it fell into despond because of a broken promise on tolls and difficulties with hospital waiting lists, Iemma expected to be a frontline casualty because the St George Hospital faced amalgamation with St Vincent's, a course resisted by both sides of the marriage and fairly well everyone in his electorate.

Bob Carr was not one to give up. He did not want to be remembered as a one-term premier. Opinion could be reversed: Carr made decisions that were deft in their capacity to win over his critics. The hospitals amalgamation was reversed. Iemma absorbed lessons on the value of a change of direction announced boldly and with minimal apology. Carr won the 1999 election with an increased majority.

The greatest threat to Iemma's advance was from within. A major stacking exercise broke out in local suburbs as Iemma and his neighbour in Lakemba, Tony Stewart MP, vied for the safe seat that was likely to emerge from the latest redistribution. That it was between two Right-wingers only added to its savagery. Iemma was offered safe passage by way of a leapfrog to Bankstown. Iemma did not entertain the possibility. Narwee and Beverly Hills were his only memories of home; he would go down rather than move. He was confident, moreover, of crushing his opponent in a preselection ballot. A peace of sorts came to pass when Head Office brokered Iemma's passage to the safe seat of Lakemba, persuading Stewart to accept the Bankstown option. They would henceforth be the other's sworn enemy. In 1999 Iemma entered the Cabinet as Minister for Public Works. It was a portfolio he relished. He could indulge in the Italian love of building big things. An election later he was handed Health. Iemma worked well with public servants and respected them for their professionalism.

New Premier, new team

Iemma was safe hands. Some time after the 2003 poll, Bob Carr was bound to announce his retirement, very likely in 2005 after he had passed Wran's record term in office. All the speculation had turned on a battle within the Right between Craig Knowles and Carl Scully. Carr was favouring Knowles and let it be known that Knowles was his only possible successor. For a number of reasons, Knowles moved out of contention. The ALP machine and a large bloc within Caucus doubted Scully had popular appeal. Iemma came into the frame, as an outsider more unlikely than likely. Not considering himself a prospect, he had not courted the media to vaunt a candidacy that did not exist. He was not making decisions with an eye to the reactions of groups within Caucus. Iemma was genuinely doubtful about taking the job, given his sense of obligation to a very young family. Talk of family is often employed in Australian politics. With Iemma it was genuine. He would resolve the problem of a man in a busy job by taking his children everywhere he could.

Although Carr's intentions were well known, his decision when it came was a surprise. The master of media management had kept his intentions to himself until he was good and ready to make his announcement and be gone. Events moved swiftly. Unlike 1986, the machine remained in the shadows. The General Secretary, Mark Arbib, did not convene meetings to talk contenders out of the contest. Arbib did talk to Right-wing MPs to let it be known the machine thought Scully was not the goods. Arbib made a case for Iemma as the most likely winner of an election post-Carr. The groupings within the Caucus, already doubtful of Scully, were hearing what they wanted to hear. A majority had lined up with Iemma not long after Carr's announcement. Arbib's most useful service to the man he championed was his anonymity. He was not seen or heard of throughout. Arbib's every activity was covert, and deniable. Realising his cause was without hope, Scully withdrew. Iemma was nominated unopposed by his faction and elected unopposed by the ALP Caucus. Iemma assumed the leadership of a government very different to the one Carr had led.

The government had already lost its Treasurer, Michael Egan, early in 2005. Egan was a man renowned for his miserable attitude toward public spending, a misery leavened by traditional Labor values and an understanding that premiers will occasionally insist on having their way. Carr and Egan had enjoyed a first class personal relationship, neither dominant of the other. When Carr refrained from blocking the long-held ministerial ambitions of Joe Tripodi as the replacement for Egan, though making it known he was unhappy to have to include him, it was the signal that Carr's own departure was imminent.

The new order persuaded Morris Iemma that the government needed to look wholly new. The persuaders prevailed on Andrew Refshauge to follow the other veterans to the door. Refshauge, formerly a medical practitioner, had been Carr's deputy for 17 years; he offered a measure of social conscience once associated with the Left. Knowles had handled a succession of portfolios well. Iemma asked Knowles to remain, an offer that Knowles declined with reluctance. Iemma's request went beyond the perfunctory and included the prospect of Treasury, a prize which both men realised was going to be difficult on the other side of impossible. Knowles had enjoyed the friendship as well as the support of Carr and Egan. He knew his treatment by Treasury under Costa would be wholly different. Knowles was at that point in a political career when his generation was passing from the scene. He looked ahead to who was taking their place: in a judgement that did not include Iemma, he did not like what he could see. How different would have been the course of events in 2007–08 if Knowles had become Treasurer back in 2005?

As late as 2005, the Labor government was relying on the personnel who arrived in the 1980s. The reconstruction of 2005 resulted in a Cabinet with a preposterous proportion of ministers coming from the Legislative Council. These MLCs, plus those ministers whose preselections depended on imposition and ongoing protection, meant a Cabinet more unconnected with the Labor Party below than any Labor government in New South Wales history. Morris Iemma, a product of the ALP branches and ALP branch culture, was the person in his own Cabinet with the unusual background. Just two decades earlier, all Labor ministers shared that background. An absence of connection with the Labor Party fuelled an ill-disguised contempt for the Labor Party and its processes.

More than new faces were part of the strategy. Iemma set about reversing decisions of the previous government, said to be hurting electorally. He altered decisions on land tax and extended assistance to licensed clubs. His Treasurer, Michael Costa, became a major player in the policy directions of the government. Major projects, announced years earlier after much planning, were abandoned. Iemma enjoyed enormous luck when John Brogden, the Opposition Leader, blooded by the 2003 campaign and now a credible threat, self-destructed after media reports of his private behaviour with journalists in a hotel – a low moment for media ethics. The source for stories of his troubles was forces within the Liberal Party. Within days Brogden felt compelled to resign and made an attempt on his own life. The new Liberal leader, Peter Debnam, was propelled to office by the same forces that had brought down Brogden. (Barry O'Farrell chose not to stand and be undermined by the same forces.) A well-marshalled religious Right had taken control of the Liberal Party machinery and was seeking to remove moderate MPs wherever they had allowed local support to slip. Factional divisions within the Liberal Party came to be reported extensively, the state of the Liberal Party was a public issue. Such material was a far more exciting story than the ongoing death of the Labor Party below.

Debnam proved to be the most inept Liberal leader in 24 years. His leadership entered slapstick when he made a commitment to have the police arrest, on the first morning after his election, some 200 young people of Middle Eastern appearance – the exact number provided – without charges and without evidence of a crime having been committed. The Police Commissioner felt the need to go on record to deny police could or would arrest anyone without cause. During the campaign Debnam promised to reduce the age of criminal liability to 10; the children convicted would go to adult prisons. Juries would determine sentences. In this burst of emotive promising on law and order, the Opposition declined to offer an alternative transport policy. Labor achieved victory in 2007 courtesy of one of the most comprehensive forfeits ever offered in Australian political history.

To ascribe the Iemma victory to forfeit alone fails to do justice to what he had achieved. His victory was the first by a premier succeeding to the job in government since Bob Heffron in long-ago 1962. He was the first Labor leader of Catholic faith to win an election since Joe Cahill in 1959. He had come a long way from his early days of hesitancy and awkwardness. The media judged Iemma against the exacting standards of Bob Carr. Iemma found that the hardest part of his new job was not the workload nor the pressure – the Health portfolio had abounded in both those challenges, in many ways more so. The hardest aspect for the new Premier was dealing with the media so as to communicate what the government was intending to do. Iemma had been a minister most attentive to detail, a fine quality in any minister but especially in spending portfolios like Health, Education and Transport. A premier has to range across all the portfolios.

Whereas Iemma as minister was devoted to studying a brief until he was its master, as a modern premier he was expected to offer responses of the instant. He found it difficult to have an opinion on everything. In the expectation that a leader has answers to everything, and cuteness to boot, being a leader of the previous Opposition confers on an election winner better preparation for the premiership than the most arduous government portfolio. There is, however, a great deal more to being a successful premier. Only four men since the end of the Second World War over 60 years earlier have taken their party into state government from Opposition – Bob Askin, Neville Wran, Nick Greiner and Bob Carr. Each had lived a life outside of parliament, bringing a wealth of experience on which they drew in tight situations. They lived an interior life as well, via reading and theatre and films – excepting Askin who invested his mind in the intricacies of form guides. There is nothing which prepares anyone for the premiership, not years of understudy, not leadership in other spheres. Putting together the building blocks of a government proceeds without a manual. Done well or done badly, the structures of government will reflect the character of the premier of the day.

Not being placed under any real pressure by the Opposition helped Iemma acquire self-confidence. So did appointments that supported Iemma's sense of what his government was about. The long-term Director-General of Premier's Department, Col Gellatly, stepped down at a time entirely of his own choosing. Gellatly's leadership had begun during the premiership of John Fahey. Iemma brought his former Director-General from Health, Robyn Kruk. He brought all the levers of the centre of government within her control when he amalgamated the Cabinet Office – an innovation of Nick Greiner – with the Premier's Department.

Another key appointment was Chief of Staff of the Premier's private office. The position did not exist until the election of Nick Greiner. Previously, premiers had been served by a small staff, aided by senior public servants and secondments. Neville Wran had operated with just two people who sat at a single desk immediately outside his cramped office in the State Office Block, plus a few others within yelling distance. That was a long way distant in 2005. On the 40th level of the Governor Macquarie Tower, a battalion served the person and the political interests of the premier of the day. A staff of that size requires leadership from one who possesses the qualities of office manager, coordinator of policy work and translator of the will of the premier. The chief of staff must have an instinctive understanding of the wishes of the premier, as well as the capacity to make a creative contribution to what those wishes might be.

The private staff of Bob Carr largely walked when Carr did. Iemma brought his loyal staff with him. The switch from heading a minister's private office to heading the premier's office is even greater for the senior staff. Recognising the inadequacies of friends is a sensitive business. Iemma decided he needed someone not connected to his ministerial career. He accepted advice that Mike Kaiser, a former Queensland MP who had been that state's ALP General Secretary, was the man designed for the task ahead. Iemma and Kaiser had become friends when Iemma was working in Canberra, a friendship reinforced by association in National Young Labor. Mark Arbib had wanted Jason Clare, an experienced staffer (later a federal MP). Though Iemma admired Clare, he wanted the person he chose, not someone whose first loyalty was bound to be to the person who landed him the job. Iemma was annoyed that Arbib let it be known the job was going to Clare. The man already in the chief's position had not expected to remain for the long haul but he was hurt to hear stories about his replacement. Iemma was denied the opportunity to break the matter gently. When the incumbent heard from the Premier who was actually taking over, he was gracious. The difficulties over staffing were not a good sign for the evolving relationship between the Premier and ALP Head Office.

Kaiser had experience as a back-to-the-wall campaigner. He brought qualities of professionalism and self-discipline, he was entirely focussed on the task of winning. To achieve that end, Kaiser would be cynical and unwavering. Kaiser was a counterfoil to Iemma's inclination to forgive human foible. The ruthless treatment of Labor MPs suffering allegations, warranted or otherwise, was following the advice of Kaiser, who would not concede an inch to distraction in any shape. An apparent presumption of guilt sundered the party.

Squandering victory from day one

The Labor victory of 2007 was one of the most remarkable in the 116 years that the party had contested New South Wales elections. A government had been re-elected after 12 years in office, its majority intact. No Australian government in recent times had approached the 16 years now certain for Labor to enjoy. The ALP had matched the mood of March 2007 perfectly by conceding serious shortcomings in the basics of state government – schools, hospitals, transport – and by promising to address those shortcomings. A slogan had been devised to connect with a public who did not want to vote for the return of the government but which could not contemplate an Opposition under such leadership – 'More to do but we're heading in the right direction'. The slogan conceded that while there was much wrong, the government deserved another chance. The resulting victory was a reprieve, not a mandate. Any relapse and the electorate would certainly deliver the demolition it had wanted to deliver.

Victory marked the moment when the good times were coming to an end. The Liberal Party had at last elected the leader it should have elected two elections earlier. The ALP Caucus elected a Cabinet that signalled of the instant that the ALP had not learned the lesson that the show was strictly probationary. According to Iemma, Arbib was determined to put into a Cabinet one Paul Gibson, an MP since 1988, a person not considered by Carr or Iemma as a prospect for promotion to the front bench in those 17 years. Iemma confronted a General Secretary who seemed beside himself to achieve this outcome. Point-blank Iemma said no. It was not the extent of the lobbying which impressed Iemma but the passion in Arbib's voice. Arbib played up contacts with the 'Left', he played every card possible. Before the factional meetings and Caucus meeting to decide the ministry, an election-winning Premier pressed for vacancies, nine new ministers and people of his own choosing. Those considered less than satisfactory or past it were moving on. There was no room even then for Gibson.

On Gibson, Mark Arbib has a strong view to the contrary. Gibson had expected to be called to the colours when Iemma assumed the premiership. He had been overlooked but thought that he had scored a promise to be next cab off the rank. In the reconstruction after the 2007 victory, Iemma was not prepared to offer Gibson a place. When Arbib made an approach on behalf of Gibson, Iemma stuck to his guns. Arbib insisted that Iemma tell Gibson face to face. At that meeting, Iemma made another promise that Gibson was next in the queue. At the eleventh hour, a serving minister surprised with an announcement of her resignation. Iemma relented with profound reluctance (by his own account); or honoured the deal he had struck with Gibson (by Arbib's).

Iemma had immediate cause for regret. On the day of the swearing-in, elements of the Caucus exploded. Allegations emerged that Gibson had committed violence against a female former MP. Iemma demanded Gibson's resignation until an inquiry resolved the matter. When that inquiry found insufficient cause to proceed, Iemma chose not to invite Gibson to return. Nor did future premiers in subsequent reshuffles.

Relations between the Premier and the ALP Head Office were becoming poisonous.

The General Secretary and strong men

The position of general secretary is vital to the success of a state Labor government in New South Wales. It is a position, full-time and well-paid, that places the occupant in charge of the party's administration. Ex officio he is campaign director for all elections in the state and principal fundraiser. The role has evolved to embrace lobbying to Labor governments on behalf of big donors to the party. The position may make the occupant a leader of the Right and a dominant voice within it. The general secretary is expected to protect the position of the Right in party ballots and preselections. The role of a general secretary requires attention to detail because his contribution, usually in deep, deniable background, augments the authority of Labor's parliamentary leader. Neutrality is not an option. An absence of support for the leader amounts to undermining the authority of the leader. A successful general secretary gets to choose the timing of his departure and in what parliament he will take a seat. Unresolvable conflict between a general secretary and a state Labor leader will mean that one or the other must depart the field.

In the 1890s and for many years, the tasks conducted by the party's central administration were minimal. The Sydney Trades and Labor Council undertook those few tasks. The Labour Leagues saw themselves as self-governing. Other than at election times, they could and did conduct their own affairs. The office of general secretary evolved out of the need to handle the paperwork generated by the leagues, maintain a register of the membership and be the point of contact between the leagues and the parliamentary Labor parties, firstly in Macquarie Street, later with the New South Wales members and senators in the Commonwealth Parliament. That officer serviced the needs of the Central Executive and became a member of it. He handled the organisational arrangements for Annual Conference. A person so well placed could and did seek to influence who was elected a delegate and the way those delegates voted. Taking control of the administration of the party office was a prize that followed the capture of the Central Executive. The workload eventually required a person employed full time, a position of considerable value when the staffs of unions were small and the political staffs of MPs and ministers did not exist. The early general secretaries did much of the office work, assisted only by stenographic and clerical persons. Beyond the office, one or two organisers covered the whole of New South Wales. The general secretary then was necessarily a powerful person, even if his power was strictly that of chief clerk.

For the first 90 years of the Labor Party in New South Wales, a strongman had regularly emerged from within the unions to rule the Right. During periods of transition from one strongman to the next, a cabal of competing strongmen exercised power not unlike the politburo of the USSR. The strongman extended his power by placing liegemen in ALP Head Office and the ACTU, by placing them in parliaments and the leadership positions of affiliated unions. Being surrounded by capable lieutenants is the essence of long-term rule. A strongman was the oracle, the settler of internal Right-wing disputes, the font of patronage, a man to be cited as being on your side. The more gifted of the strongmen ensured that many others enjoyed a place in the sun. The strongman was strong because he delivered rewards within his gift to those who were loyal.

A strongman emerging from the unions became less likely as unions lost their social relevance. Big unions became ill-fitting combinations of industries and callings, a chance of faction and personality, driven by the political class for the political class. The governance of the industrial side of the ALP evolved from a prince in the Labor Council ruling the principality to a coalition of barons enjoying irresistible powers within their own private baronies. The barons contested hegemony without necessarily acknowledging the principality of the prince. With the creation of monster unions, baronies enjoy abundant resources and staff, a potential for power at least the equivalent of the once all-powerful Labor Council – which now goes by the cuddly name of Unions NSW. The monolithic Right has developed minor cracks as warring tribes have fought for dominance, expressed in the ability to advance their officials and liegemen into the Senate, Legislative Council and safe seats. The hatred between, for example, the (Right-wing) Transport Workers' Union and the (Right-wing) Australian Workers' Union is sulphuric. Containing such acute hatreds is a major challenge for the leadership of the Right. Exit points for the disaffected and the disappointed have decreased: arbitration commissions and industrial courts, the location of some of the plummest, well-paid, even titled jobs in times past, have disappeared.

The ALP General Secretary and the Secretary of Unions NSW need to be allies to manage Right-wing ambition. The first principle of the Right's management is to ensure that, however bitter the conflict within the faction, the warring parties remain united against the 'Left'. It says much about the character of the Right that virtually all intra-factional contests conclude with a united front. The weakness of the 'Left' has made differences within the Right more deadly. The balance of power between the factions is shattered, the Right is overwhelmingly dominant, one or both sides of the 'Left' are supplicants for favours, the temptation to treat the party as the property of faction is strong.

John Ducker

Diffusion of contemporary power makes unlikely the re-emergence of a strongman. The last strongman was John Ducker, NSW President from 1971 to 1979. A migrant from Yorkshire, Ducker had risen from the foundry floor through the ranks of the Ironworkers' Association to a position of control in the Labor Council. A force in all spheres of the NSW and national Right, Ducker was, most obviously, the ruler of Labor Council. His power with affiliated unions made him the ruler of the ALP in New South Wales, a power in the ALP National Executive and the ACTU. His influence flowed everywhere. Ducker was also a part-time MLC in that enlightened era when MLCs were not a part of the state parliamentary Labor Party. Ducker was a source of advice and a background general in the affairs of the state Caucus. Ducker reckoned early that Labor could not win under Patrick Darcy Hills. His eye fell on Neville Wran, a leading Labor lawyer, ambitious but with the gift of patience. Note how important it is for a machine leader to identify potential leaders who can win elections.

In the benighted world of federal Labor in the 1960s, Ducker was one who had judged Gough Whitlam to be the hope of the party nationally. The NSW Right backed Whitlam. They made him their favourite son though, in truth, Whitlam was not one of them. Ducker backed Whitlam when backing him made strategic sense. Ducker kept backing Whitlam when the wheels began to fall off after 1975. Whitlam could not have survived the Iraqi loans affair of 1976 nor the challenge of Bill Hayden in 1977 without Ducker's unstinting support.

Ducker was wise enough to know that his power was stronger if left unstated. His power grew with each decisive revelation of support for a winner. Ducker was adept at speaking in a lowered voice in a Yorkshire accent, tone steady, slowly explaining the consequences for action unwelcome, all of it implied. After an almost casual recital, he would add: 'and that's not a threat but a promise'. His stock phrase to a Right-winger contemplating independence was succinct: 'In that case, we will have to look into your situation'. Said would-be rebel needed to be leading an unblemished life with a hold over his union or electorate beyond the reach of the Labor Council, otherwise the would-be was going to experience life in all its richness.

When Ducker departed, very suddenly, in 1979, his various positions were split many ways. Graham Richardson became the Right's delegate to the National Executive, Paul Keating became ALP President, Barrie Unsworth became Secretary of the Labor Council. Keating's focus remained on the national Parliament. He had accepted the presidency to assist his faction at a time of great need. Richardson, by dint of Keating's indifference, applied his mind to the small picture of disputes and credentials and who was winning the local electorate councils. This was the first instance of Keating preferring the big picture. No union official nor occupant of the post of president has since approached the extent of Ducker's authority. It is unlikely anyone ever will.

Career path

The general secretary has usually emerged from within the ranks of the ALP Head Office staff. The future leader of the party machine is expected to learn the ropes in the lowly world of party organiser, a job involving much travel, many meetings, distasteful activity and unquestioning support for orders from above. In the 1970s the party office professionalised. Employment provided excellent prospects of a career that would end in parliament for those who had been successful, according to the performance indicators enunciated by the Right – an ability to win general elections and deliver control of annual conference. In later years the ability to raise funds for the party became important.

The General Secretary during the transition to professionalism was Peter Westerway (1969–73), previously an academic and television reporter. He was not comfortable in the post, not understanding the powers inherent to it. Westerway's real interest was election campaigns and finding a seat for himself. To run for the Senate in a loseable position, Westerway resigned his party office. When he missed out, he had lost his power base for future claims. No later general secretary has accepted a spot on the Senate ticket other than number one.

Geoff Cahill (1973–76) was a brutal authoritarian while an aspirant who converted to being inclusive when he reached the top job. By reaching out when in charge of the party machine, by questioning the authority of John Ducker, Cahill made himself a hostage to fortune. Unwise use of a credit card while in the United States provided the smoking gun needed to organise Cahill's purging, a surgical exercise without a public dimension, planned and executed in total secrecy. Cahill had signed his resignation before the party learned their General Secretary was in trouble. The Labor Council had provided proof – if proof were necessary – that they controlled the Right. What was so in 1976 is not so now.

Cahill's successor was Graham Richardson (1976–83). With the departure of Ducker he defined the modern role for a general secretary as the principal source of authority within the Right. Richardson had begun as an organiser and done all that was necessary to lay claim to promotion positions as they arose. His first employment by the ALP required him to be a bovver boy – an enforcer and a whip, the wielder of language to lacerate, the ability to mock opponents, be unfair and misrepresent. The young man on the rise is expected to provide thrills for his side, occasion boos from the other. Amid the clowning is the serious purpose of watching what is happening in branches, checking unwelcome developments, having eyes and ears for what is happening. Come the ballots and key floor votes at conference, the party organiser is expected to deliver a maximum vote by whatever means are available. Every party organiser since Graham Richardson has been an imitation, pale or otherwise.

Richardson built the authority of the office of general secretary, the first to realise its full potential. The general secretary would be manager of the office, the efficiency of which was always a matter of doubt. With a stream of visitors, reaching out by phone and personal visits, the general secretary was the key source of advice for operatives involved in combat with the 'Left' and the provider of assistance in credentialing and ballots. The general secretary tried to sort out differences within the Right so as to earn the allegiances of both sides. Increasingly he was a public identity, prominent in the media, sometimes notorious. Most of all he was responsible for maintaining the Right's control of the ALP in New South Wales by ensuring the delegations sent to conference by unions, electorate councils and other bodies favoured the Right.

Stephen Loosley, General Secretary from 1983 to 1990, had been induced to defect from the Left by Richardson. He loved to be loathed by his one-time allies. Loathed he was. Loosley made it into the Senate, but was soon a casualty of problems with a building purchased by the NSW Branch on his watch. Expecting to be a minister and a force in a federal Labor government, he was only ever a bit player. John Della Bosca (1990–99) then, now, always, was liked by all. Without enemies of note, 'Della' was on track to become ALP national president when he forgot that a conversation with Maxine McKew, then of *The Bulletin*, was on the record. Similarly, his fine service as a state minister counted for little, not against other mishaps also involving women.

Eric Roozendaal (1999–2004) loved the theatre of conflict. He loved a stoush. Whereas Richardson recognised that a general secretary had to transcend his past, Roozendaal did not entertain that possibility. In 2003 he was responsible for a swathe of impositions for safe seats in the Legislative Assembly. Roozendaal's insistence at the 2003 Annual Conference that Steve Hutchins would take top spot on the Senate ticket (ahead of John Faulkner, Labor's Senate leader) pressed to the limit the authority of the general secretary. Pressed though it was, the authority remained intact. The general secretary rules or the general secretary falls.

Mark Arbib (2004–07) was the most powerful occupant of the office since Richardson. General Secretary at the beginning of Iemma's leadership, the two men considered the other to be a friend and confidant, a relationship that extended to Arbib's successor, Karl Bitar. Each of the general secretaries from Richardson to Arbib had worked their way from the lowliest post in the machine. Their orderly succession meant that each general secretary was followed by his assistant, with the next in line already chosen. For 32 years the leadership succession in the NSW Right was a model for management.

Arbib, however, had left office without leaving behind his leadership of the Right. He maintained an intense interest in factional affairs. Arbib's ongoing involvement and the expectations that Iemma, Arbib and Bitar held of each other, would be key factors in the Iemma leadership after the triumph of the 2007 state election. The three men enjoyed friendships of long, long standing. Friendship was friendship. That was the past. Politics alone would define their ongoing relationships.

Electricity: The government killer

There was a problem for a Labor government in attempting to sell the electricity industry. That problem was Labor policy. The party's policy on power generation required public ownership of the plant and facilities for generating electricity, public ownership of the transmission lines, public ownership of the corporations that charge for supply. Such a policy was an inconvenience if you were a treasurer who believed that these assets should be sold so as to release the capital locked in ownership.

Michael Costa is the son of Greek immigrants, a minister in a government which had an attractive back-story of a first generation of Australian-born children of migrant parents. He had attended Ibrox Park Boys High in Leichhardt, a tough school for a tough lad. Costa had worked in a variety of places, including driving a locomotive. He had won office in that union. Once a Trotskyist, he had become a disciple of free-market economist Friedrich von Hayek. Costa was part of a school of thought that believes the state should not be involved in the market in any form. Through the agency of the ALP, the train drivers' union and the Labor Council of New South Wales, Costa had made a rise uninterrupted while espousing views that had been anathema to mainstream Labor for most of the party's existence. Costa was the most committed child of the economic reforms of the 1980s, a true believer in market forces uninterrupted by regulation. Few Liberals share the purity of his passion for a market economy in which taxes are light and falling, the hand of government is stayed, public services are at best a necessary evil compelled by a failure in the market. Costa was a man who believed powerfully in what he believed. He did not brook opposition. His method of arguing crossed the border into bullying. The sale of electricity assets was a matter he not so privately supported when he was an official of the Labor Council in 1997 and was necessarily rendered silent. Costa pursued the opportunity for the sale in 2008 like a man whose hour had arrived. Morris Iemma gave Costa his head.

Iemma had come to believe in the same cause: he was impressed by the numbers on generating capacity, advice coming out of Treasury and the national regulator that New South Wales would not be able to meet its base-load capacity by 2014. The short-term needs were dealt with by building three new power stations. Iemma took the view that the solution was dictated by the nature of the electricity market. Electricity generation was a national market, primarily operated by private owners. Capital markets would fund power stations only in circumstances that made the investment worth the while of private operators and investors. The government believed the viability of the existing electricity business was in doubt. Public retailers in a private market were severely constrained. To keep stations in public ownership was going to cost $3 billion. Bills for refurbishing and new construction would come to $15 billion. There was a limit to the state's borrowing capacity. The government had already embarked on a massive infrastructure spend.

In Iemma's view, once there was a national market, the days were numbered for state-owned stations. For a Premier recently re-elected with an ambitious program for health and infrastructure, not spending that quantum on capital works for electricity in favour of spending the proceeds of a sale became irresistible. The Premier was prepared to place his authority on the line with a view to using *force majeure* to drive the sale through all obstacles. The logic of this course the Premier considered irresistible. Unfortunately, much of his party was determined to resist.

Overturning ALP policy on long-cherished beliefs had become familiar, most recently in the economic reforms that opened the Australian economy to global forces during the Hawke–Keating era. None of them had a basis in ALP policy. The leadership of the Hawke government went to successive National Conferences to seek approval for changes to ALP policy that enabled those governments to proceed with widespread privatisation of tranches of Qantas and the Commonwealth Bank. Hawke, Keating and colleagues did not entertain the notion they could act contrary to ALP policy. The Left of the time spluttered all the way to the edge of a cliff, voted no, lost the vote – and walked away from the cliff. Iemma was entitled to believe he could achieve all or most of what he wanted by demanding the party examine its policies.

The long decade of the Howard government sold off what remained of the family silver. During that same decade in the states, Labor and conservative governments introduced competition in utilities like water and electricity. State ownership of banks and insurance companies ceased. Fabulous prices were extracted for TABs. Electricity and water were a special case. The distribution of water and electricity proceed along the same wires or channels, the product for sale is identical whatever brand it carries, whatever price charged. (This author served as a director of one of the electricity supply companies.) The great battles for market share were shams by grown men and women as they cased customers and set prices. The prices on offer to the big plants were blind auctions in reverse, guesswork about hair-thin margins or loss leaders as the price for bragging rights about market share. The effect of market competition was to drive down the price of electricity unreasonably. A regulator kept it down. By 2010, prices to consumers were rising sharply, partly in recognition that prices had been ridiculously low for too long. A sustained increase in the price of electricity will be a feature of the Australian economy for an indefinite period.

The winners of that period were the electricity companies that sat on their hands and disregarded market share. The reward for the successful was being gouged by the NSW Treasury for higher dividends, on top of the payment of the equivalence of income tax. Treasury's trick was to shift state debt off the books of the state by means of loading electricity companies with responsibility for paying interest on debt that the electricity companies did not incur. A real company will incur debt because it has invested in plant and equipment. The corporatised electricity companies in state ownership had loads of debt imposed which were a fiction in terms of productive potential but no less horribly real in terms of the cash outflow by way of interest payable that the debt dictated.

The government had been drawing down big dollars from the electricity companies. The quantum was not enough for the government. Not even with the equivalent of income tax, plus dividends, plus special dividends imposed at the Treasury's pleasure, plus interest paid to the government for debt that the same government had off-loaded onto the companies' books. The flow of cash by 2008 was not sufficient, the government said.

The Carr government had been seeking to release the capital locked up in the state's electricity assets from the moment that Michael Egan took over Treasury in 1995. In 1997, Egan made a valiant effort, supported by his Premier. The effort failed. Annual Conference was going to reject the privatisation proposal by an overwhelming margin, so overwhelming that the tacticians for the government decided not to press for a vote. Eleven years later, Morris Iemma was insisting privatisation would proceed. The party would have to change its policy.

The approach Iemma pursued was a model that was least offensive to the ALP. He began taking soundings after the state election, before he began the formal process. The formal process began with the Cabinet decision that triggered the Owen Inquiry. He encountered no significant opposition to the retail companies being sold, though those soundings had not included the union covering the retail workers. Nor was there opposition to the private sector building the new generators. Iemma's broad plan kept 100 per cent of the generators and transmission lines in public ownership. He took soundings on a measure whereby the government leased the generators so they could be upgraded. The proceeds were marked for capital works and social programs thought to be attractive to union leaders. The initial reactions were guarded but supportive, Iemma has recalled, provided the generators were not being sold.

The Owen Inquiry took public submissions. Iemma continued with soundings during and after. Over the passing months the Premier of New South Wales was involved in over a hundred meetings, some of considerable duration, many taxing, essentially with the union leadership of his own party. Views necessarily differ about whether a consensus emerged and whether there was ever any prospect of agreeing to the government's plans. In short, sale of retail was likely okay, the sale of generators was not.

Discussions turned on how best to look after union members, talks that embraced protections and job guarantees, regional employment, regional offices. Iemma believed he had agreement on protection for price increases, jobs and the environment. Legislation was promised expressly to provide 100 per cent ownership of the generators. Roundtables proceeded one after another with Unions NSW, various ministers, union officials and delegations of union officials. Sometimes Costa was present, sometimes he was not. In private, union officials were frank. They were formally opposed but would accept whatever ALP President Bernie Riordan found acceptable. Solidarity dictated the support outside the electricity industry for the campaign of unions inside it.

The inability to nail down an agreement that Iemma thought was within reach was frustrating the Premier. 'The matter had to come to a landing', Iemma insisted. Electricity was dominating Iemma's time. A perception developed that the Premier was distracted, other areas of government had lost impetus because no one was driving any other agenda. Kaiser had departed in December 2007, an important loss. Legislation promised in other areas was not emerging, the time and resources of Parliamentary Counsel (the unit responsible for drafting legislation) was consumed by the electricity bills. Instructions to out-source drafting of other measures did not have a result. There were those in his government who took advantage of his distraction to do as they preferred, or do nothing they did not want to.

As months went by, Iemma believed that the unions were going back on statements made to him. Differences became public, a campaign developed about electricity. Trust disappeared. Against a deteriorating political background, the future of the electricity industry had become an issue of political badinage. Iemma found himself playing a hand based on the intricacies of sale and the benefits that might flow against opponents who were invoking ALP policy. Iemma's strategic error was not taking his cause beyond the closed meetings of union officials into the ranks of the party below. The process of closed discussion reinforced a perception held by the party membership that the leadership took them for granted. The union leadership contrived to become the champions of party membership and a meaningful role for the party. Unions posturing on behalf of ALP democracy was rich indeed.

An all but final attempt at an agreement was the creation of a committee headed by Barrie Unsworth – former Premier, former Secretary of Labor Council and former official of the Electrical Trades Union. Affiliated unions were represented. The committee's purpose was to check the proposals emerging from the government against the requirements of the ALP platform. It found the proposals conformed with the platform. Union members issued a dissenting report.

Supporters of the government position took a legalistic comfort in those findings. The findings of the Unsworth committee changed nothing for reason that the managers of Conference were determined that only Annual Conference could provide the ticks that an earlier Annual Conference had required. In the governance of NSW Labor, Conference (being sovereign) could change the rules of the game even as it was being played. The Right, joined in this enterprise by their factional opponents, did not much care about such fineries. Only Conference could give the go-ahead to a sale.

The modern parliamentary leader

Every aspect of a modern party is built around projecting the image of the parliamentary leadership. The parliamentary leader has become the party's face to the electorate. In the absence of an internal culture, parties depend on leaders to define whatever they are. A template defines the parliamentary leader: they are deemed wise and strong if they compel their party to offer obeisance to their will – however whimsical, wrong-headed, ill-considered or unresearched. Leaderships must prevail over their own parties in the event of conflict or a leadership is deemed to have failed. No credit goes to leaders who consult with the party membership. Being persuaded by your own party members of the wrongness of a course is a sign of weakness. Feeling bound by a pledge to honour what you are pledged to honour, that is a sign of weakness. Strength equals disdain for those who are your stalwart supporters. Leadership is demonstrated by responding to headlines, opinion polls, splashes of shock and horror.

Criticism from within the ALP is welcome background noise, affirmation that the ALP leader is bigger than his party, a leader for all, not some. No small part of the tragedy for Morris Iemma, a leader of the most traditional kind – of and from the ranks – is that he allowed himself to be positioned as the enemy of party tradition and principle. His total belief in the rightness of his cause had blinded him to the hostility of the party below to what he was proposing. Though he had an incontrovertible case that an ALP Conference was unrepresentative of both the Labor Party and Labor voters, like all of his predecessors, he had not publicly denounced its unrepresentative structure nor previously denied its legitimacy. Unions controlled the Conference. That was the problem for Iemma. It was not a problem suddenly arising.

The structural problem of an unrepresentative conference was a problem pressing and immediate because unions opposed the privatisation of the electricity industry. As 2007 became 2008, Bernie Riordan continued to oppose. So did Unions NSW, led by John Robertson – a strategic thinker who could see the long game amid the rhetoric. Opposition from the President of the ALP and the Secretary of Unions NSW translated into a united bloc from the Right-wing unions and the delegates from the Right-wing electorate councils. That would make a substantial majority on the floor of Conference before you even counted the delegates from the 'Left', who would be voting against privatisation by reflex. To overcome the unrepresentative nature of Conference was going to require years of courageous advocacy and provided no guarantee of a different outcome, not without a massive investment of time in educating branch activists on the merits of sale. The recent precedent of Simon Crean, who perished partly in the cause of party reform, was not encouraging for a potential reformer.

A direct appeal to the delegates, minus a plea to address the structure of Conference, would go nowhere with delegates whose first loyalty was to the factions who were a large part of the reason they were delegates. Iemma, by necessity, felt compelled to stick to the tried and true formula of a parliamentary leader thwarted in his ambitions – keep talking to union officials until such time as combinations of seduction and cajolery convinced the unions that there was something for everyone in the arrangement. That process served to reinforce the perception of a party leadership seeking a fix and a dominant Right faction prepared to deal on any matter. As the rhetoric escalated and gained extensive media attention, the prospect of retreat became even more damaging to both sides.

Both Riordan and Robertson had once worked in the electricity industry. Robertson did not conform to expectations on matters of policy. When the arrival of refugees was a frontline issue in 2001 and 2002, Robertson had supported their arrival. He was a leading force in a coalition of ALP members who supported the refugees. Most of his fellow Labor for Refugees members were from what there remained of an ALP Left. Robertson, a leader of the Right, provided lessons in the basics of persuasion. Basic political sense: never call those who disagree with us racists. We who are in this coalition cannot win the coming debate if we offend those we are seeking to convert. He was to apply the same coalition-building moderation in the campaign against WorkChoices.

On electricity privatisation, Unions NSW was taking a position supported by every union affiliated to it. Not one union spoke up for privatisation in the councils of unions nor inside the ALP. What happened behind closed doors remained behind those doors. The vast majority of the ALP membership continued to oppose electricity privatisation. Exactly one state electorate council voted in favour. A Labor government can ignore branches and the membership, it cannot ignore union officials.

Opponents were not minded to abandon party policy – a definition which they controlled, as to the mechanism that did the defining. They were minded to enforce their definition. For those who had seen union posturing against the policies of Labor governments many times over the decades, there was every reason to believe opposition to electricity privatisation was another shadow play – look good for the troops, fold with concessions, be mollified with weasel words of respect for those who folded after the rhetoric had played. Such plays had worked a treat through the 1980s and 1990s.

A good question was why Riordan and co had not exercised their undoubted majority on the ALP Administrative Committee to schedule Annual Conference months earlier so as to lay down the law to the Premier. Why were they not asserting that control? The Treasurer, Michael Costa, had made it clear he was not going to continue inside a government that squibbed privatisation. Bernie Riordan was in equal earnest about stopping privatisation. The opponents of privatisation could not stop privatisation unless prepared to bring down the Premier. Or was it the other way around? Was the main game the purging of Iemma? Certainly, Iemma came to believe that was why he could not nail down agreement even when differences appeared settled.

Elements of the Iemma government floated the notion to friendly reporters that it might not bother to persuade the Annual Conference. If this were true, the gambit amounted to an attempted coup of breathtaking proportions. The threat was the government would achieve its ambitions ahead of Conference by pre-emption, afterwards by naked defiance. The perception the government was bent on sale, regardless of the decision of Conference, was devastating to the case for sale. A big loss on the floor of Conference turned into a rout once delegates from the electorate councils realised the government was saying the party did not matter. It did not matter that Iemma did not believe he had said any such thing.

For Iemma the consequences were becoming terminal. He was aware what the issue had become. Will the Premier stare down a conference? He was prepared to introduce the bills come what may, regardless of the Pledge. The by-play of meetings without end had taken him past a point of no return. 'I had been wrestling with smoke for eight months', Morris Iemma told me, 'then I felt there had been a very deliberate rejection of two compromises which gave the unions exactly what they wanted'.

The details of all that happened are intricate. One compromise, Iemma told this author, was characterised by Riordan as being exactly what the unions had offered Carr and Egan in 1997 and which they had rejected. Riordan chortled at the rich irony of such an outcome. Iemma believed he had reached a deal, then found Riordan disowned what he had agreed to. Riordan and Robertson have expressly denied to this author any such exchange and deny that any arrangement offered by the government was like 1997.

Riordan and Robertson, in return, recollected a deal worked out in mid-2007 with Della Bosca and Ian Macdonald that involved selling one power station in a public float with a cornerstone of 20 per cent reserved for industry superannuation funds. The proposal was delivered by Della Bosca to the Premier and the Treasurer. For his troubles, as told by Riordan and Robertson, Della Bosca was thrown out of Iemma's office. Morris Iemma has rebutted that assertion with a detailed account of what Della Bosca was proposing. Iemma rejected the proposal because he thought it 'a complete dud – confused, convoluted and not achieving our objective of securing new baseload investment'. Cursory dismissal was all that it warranted. Della Bosca had acted beyond his authority, one more action that caused Iemma to doubt where Della Bosca's loyalties lay. The delivery and swift rebuttal fitted perfectly the allegation that Iemma was not interested in a deal. Without humour in his chuckle, Iemma noted that he was being belted for a package that involved 100 per cent of the generators remaining in public ownership while his opponents in the unions, the orchestrators of the criticism, were proposing to sell a proportion of the generators.

Another story, related by Mark Arbib, is that one week out from Conference, he and Bitar met Riordan and Robertson to achieve a compromise. A deal was struck. Bitar took the deal to Iemma, who agreed. Arbib arranged for Riordan to meet the Prime Minister so as to gain the seal of approval from that quarter. Iemma took the deal to Costa, who also agreed. All that is certain is that a deal on which the principals thought there was agreement was dead. No one can explain where it went wrong. The meeting with the Prime Minister proceeded, though it was without relevance to privatisation.

In these stories there are conflicting versions on every key detail though, mercifully, the participants agree that an exchange along these broad outlines did happen. These accounts are just two that emerged from the more than one hundred meetings during 2007 and 2008. Those meetings were sometimes formal, with public servants present and a record taken, sometimes informal. Some were secret, some were meetings that 'did not happen'. Before the meetings and immediately after, exchanges took place more important than anything at the meetings. Chance encounters led to critical discussions and renewed hopes of a compromise. Colossal numbers of telephone calls explored nuances and brought a curt end to renewed hope.

The by-plays of accusation, denial and counter-accusation are worthy of extensive treatment in a book about the attempt to privatise electricity in New South Wales. To explore every exchange between the principals alone, without considering the many other players, will take this book away from the story of why a premier was brought down by his own party.

Morris Iemma has remained convinced that the vote at Conference was not about electricity or the Platform. His opponents do not disagree that there was a larger agenda. They emphatically disagree that they were not interested in compromise or that at any stage they agreed to any proposition offered by the government. What was absent was an honest broker, universally respected, who could put together a deal acceptable to all parties or, apprehending a deal was not possible, call the two sides together to declare emphatically that the deal was undoable. No one could declare the war over, not until only one army remained on the field.

Chapter 4
Annual Conference, May 2008

Critics of ALP Conferences are correct that modern governments cannot have a mere thousand people issuing instructions to an elected government. These critics of union control and conference sovereignty found their voices so very late. Those who denounced the unions exercising their formal voting strength on the floor of Conference were a galaxy of those who had benefited from the union bloc vote throughout their careers. Bob Carr, Barrie Unsworth and Paul Keating were vocal that unions were not entitled to dictate to an elected government. In set-piece offerings they denied the legitimacy of a conference decision that was adverse to the wishes of the government. None of these former leaders had been shy about demanding the support of the bloc vote to back in their enterprises in times past.

It was fine and good for unions to have untrammelled power on the floor of Conference when they delivered what governments wanted; it was an outrage when unions were in earnest about matters inconvenient to government. Bob Carr had not wavered in his support for union bloc control of the ALP Conference during his 17 years as party leader. A handful of union officials had always delivered what he wanted – bar electricity privatisation. Persuading the representatives of the party membership was a less certain, more demanding affair. The membership had to cop whatever an inner group of Right union officials found acceptable. At a time when there was a prospect of diminishing union power, Carr, a long-time beneficiary of union control of the ALP, had spoken in favour of continuing control of the party by the sliver of unions which remained affiliated to the ALP. He and the other fair-weather supporters of union control were advocating a protection racket: unions are legitimate only as and when they provide a leave pass for all that Labor governments might do.

It was rich beyond words to hear protests from ministers and former ministers about Conference reminding a government of its place in the Labor Party. Protesters from within the parliamentary party especially lacked the faculty for recognising who and what they were – and who had made them what they were. Conferences had selected all the members of the Legislative Council. Increasingly, Conferences had sanctioned interventions in preselections so as to overwhelm the views of locals and install favoured sons and daughters. Conference had protected the favoured against challenge and protected the favoured from the consequences of their follies. By 2008, the ranks of the Iemma government and the state parliamentary party were a translation of conference operatives of the recent past. No Labor Caucus had been so dominated by members dependent on their ongoing loyalty to the factions outside the parliament.

It was these same Conferences which, through the last twenty years or so, had elected the members of the Administrative Committee, the Review Tribunal, Credentials Committee and Disputes Committee who had provided the wilful decisions or the blind eye to the rorts and the stacking, the slide into sharp practices, the destruction of critical thinking, the elevation of liegemen whose lack of competence was not a material consideration – the death below.

Because of electricity, the ALP in New South Wales was entering a state of affairs not seen since the mid-1980s when the Left disappeared – two sides to a debate who believed what they were saying. The customary set-piece imposture – lip-service opposition followed by meek acquiescence – remained the expectation right up to conference eve. In the living memory of all participants, the unions had always folded or the government had walked away to fight another day. Avoiding an open clash between the machine and the party in government was the one point of strategy on which decades of hard men had been able to agree. Would 2008 be different?

If Conference, duly constituted, voted against a change of policy and, in a mood of defiance, carried a resolution expressly opposing privatisation, that had to be the end of the matter. That was the end of the matter for Bob Carr and Michael Egan who, though mightily unimpressed, folded their tents when the Conference turned down privatisation in 1997. Carr won his first re-election in 1999 by taking the side of the angels against a wicked Coalition which was proposing privatisation. The government failed to address the alleged importance of the proposed sale in each of the years from 1998 to 2007. Carr scored a handsome majority in 1999 by espousing opposition to what he had personally supported. Carr repeated that victory in 2003 with express opposition to the sale of electricity. Iemma won in 2007 with a silence on electricity that could only mean its sale was not on the agenda. The government dared not claim a mandate for sale.

> Discounting their rancor, there is no trump card in using the supremacy of the ALP state conference in May to block the sale. These are the realities that the unions must face up to. And there are signs that this is already happening at the top. Unions boss John Robertson's delegation of comment on the issue to his deputy Mark Thistlewaite [sic: Matt Thistlethwaite] is a clear sign of this resignation.
>
> (Simon Benson, *Daily Telegraph*, 13 Feb 2008)

For the first time Right-wing members of the Labor Caucus were discovering what it meant to deal with a deck stacked against them. They were facing the novelty of a situation beyond the manipulative telephone call, a sweetheart deal, the clever fix. Instead, the formal authority of Conference was going to be exercised without finesse against their express wishes. None of which mattered, it seemed. The government was not for bending. As Conference was preparing to meet, events were moving beyond control.

Extremism was coming into the open. A critical mass of Labor MPs in both Houses made it clear they were prepared to vote against any legislation contrary to Labor policy. A party officer, Luke Foley, encouraged MPs to cross the floor of Parliament and be proclaimed by history's judgement as Labor heroes. Foley occupied the one paid position for the 'Left' on the staff of the ALP in New South Wales. Foley was an important player in the politics of electricity, for reason that the Right was traumatised about opposing their own. During 2007 and 2008, the Right and 'Left' officials of the party could and did work as one because everyone in the office was genuinely of one view. Foley had no doubts about the proper course of action. His certainty made him a leader of the movement against privatisation. None of his predecessors on the Left or 'Left' had enjoyed the influence he was about to exercise.

> Mr Iemma said he did not believe he needed confer-
> ence approval to press ahead with the electricity sale
> because the matter had been to cabinet and caucus
> and the former premier, Barrie Unsworth, who had run
> a committee with the unions on the matter, had deter-
> mined he was not breaching the party platform by
> pressing ahead.
>
> (Andrew Clennell, *SMH*, 19 April 2008)

With all hope of compromise gone, a hardline motion was going to Conference to instruct the government not to introduce the electricity legislation. Unnoted, the resolution also conferred on the General Secretary the authority to do all that was necessary to stop the legislation. The campaign against electricity privatisation continued to be the public backdrop to the inexorable demolition of Iemma's standing. John Robertson stepped back from being the unions' spokesman, a deliberate decision to avoid his persona becoming the issue. Given the parliamentary press gallery, it was a wise precaution. Stepping back did not provide him leave in the personalised reporting that followed.

Conference convenes

The NSW Labor Annual Conference met on 3–4 May 2008. For the first time in over 50 years the Sydney Town Hall was not available, owing to a major refurbishment. Since 1954, the Annual Conference has met in the upper hall of the city council's place of business. All those long weekends for year upon year, the shuffling in and out, the rituals of dining and coffee, made the Sydney Town Hall seem like the home of the ALP in conference. The geography of the alcoves, wings, galleries, side rooms, space beneath the stage, the tiered seating for the choir – each element dictated the rhythms of an ALP Conference. The seats on the floor were flexible. Rows could be as deep or as wide as management might manipulate. The Sydney Town Hall was a first-class lesson in the geography of power, the anthropology of groups. All that was gone. The 2008 conference was staged in the main auditorium of the Sydney Convention Centre.

The Convention Centre can be entered from several directions. The preferred entrance proved to be via the steps facing Darling Harbour. There assembled the protesters in their yellow T-shirts opposed to the sale of electricity. Inside, equal participation was not possible, mobility was near zero. Take a seat and you were anchored. Be in the middle of a row and you were entrapped. The only lecterns were on the stage, you had to get on a speakers' list. For the first time ever, the electorate council delegations were split: manipulation of the crudest kind, what happens when boys get to play. At a conference in which any sort of factional loyalty was in play, physically concentrating the factions would have concentrated the disaffected. A concentration of hostility made no sense from a management point of view.

Starting time was 9:00. The actual start was closer to 9:30, with an Aboriginal welcome to country. Booklets containing the official business of Conference lay in plastic folders on the floor in front of the seats of delegates. (ALP Rules require the business papers be posted to delegates eight weeks before Conference; such a breach would occasion no sanction.) ALP policy on selling public assets was worth re-reading, inserted by the 1997 Conference on a motion of John Della Bosca. The plain meaning of the text and the 12-point criteria made it clear that the tick for the government to proceed had to come from the body that established the criteria. That body is the Annual Conference. The government could not give itself a tick.

The atmosphere and all else was so different to the Town Hall in June. In the decades when winters were cold, we had known and come to love the roof radiators and the omnipresence of cigarette smoke, the lovely old organ, the balconies on three sides looking down, the stage at the front at a level well above the body of the hall, tiered seating behind where only big shots dared to tread. Town Hall facilitated a conference; Darling Harbour provided seats for an audience.

Two cameras recorded proceedings. The media were in two galleries at right-angles to the stage, the television cameras to the right of the stage. The cameras occasionally panned around to capture colour. Many seats were unoccupied. The composition seemed a reasonable cross-section of generations and genders. Plenty were wearing yellow T-shirts handed out by the ETU.

The press gallery misses the point

Reporters covering state politics have offices in Parliament House. They tend to be organised in bureaux according to the proprietor of their masthead or call sign. These reporters are dependent on the drip that comes out of the Government and the Opposition. These reporters lack knowledge of New South Wales political history. Any insight and acuity is supplied by sources, or is missing. The Carr government elevated to an art form the importance of meeting the needs of these reporters by providing them with exclusives. There was a bargain unspoken. Squaring the media did not begin with Carr. In his memoir on the Wran era, Brian Dale (Wran's press secretary from opposition into the halcyon years of government) explained how television reporters were provided with juicy stories as they were approaching negotiations about their contract renewal. The bargain did not have to be spoken.

No longer do trade unions warrant a separate round of industrial reporters based at the Trades Hall. The parliamentary round once had to countenance industrial reporters well informed about the machinations of the Labor Party, because the industrial reporters were covering the offices of unions and the Labor Party in and around the Trades Hall. The industrial reporters were hardened and knowledgeable. They knew their round. That meant knowing the Labor Party. Industrial reporters tended to be sympathetic to unions, which was why they built a range of sources among union officials. Those blokes picked up good exclusives. For stories on the Labor Party outside Parliament – which is most of the Labor Party – the ALP machine and the competing factions worked the industrial roundsmen. They may have been biased but they knew their stuff. You could not bedazzle them with fantasy.

In the 1970s, the Trades Hall was blessed with veterans who knew their stuff, inheritors of a proud tradition. Fred Wells (*Herald*, an ex-comm, and ASIO informant we learned after he died), Joe Buchanan (*Sun*), Jack Simpson (*Telegraph*) and Ray Turner (*Daily Mirror*) revered the Labor Party of old. Neal Swancott (*The Australian*) was a boy in this company but he knew his round. If they were still around when the boys in Macquarie Street fell so badly for the government line, you would have heard the old industrial flacks yelling down the phones to the newsrooms: 'The stories are nonsense. Iemma's not calling the shots here.' (Their language might have enjoyed a sprinkling of salt.)

Instead, in the modern era, state parliamentary reporters perceive all stories through a Macquarie Street perspective. Political parties enter the story as an interest group. The separate lives of parties warrant treatment as a catchment for parliament. Parties tend to be reported only when in scandal or violent division. Neither newspapers nor the broadcast media have the staff, the researchers, the fact-checkers or the sub-editors to ensure stories have a semblance of accuracy. Given that the editorial leadership favoured privatisation of electricity, exaggerations in support of that cause had an easy passage.

A Macquarie Street outlook, combined with hostility to unionism, made for a one-sided story about confrontations between unions and government. The attempt to sell the electricity assets of New South Wales provided a romantic tale about a brave government determined to stare down dictation by unelected people from a party machine which was itself nothing more than the creature of unions. For the reporting of this tale, the News Limited bureau in Parliament House has any number of reporters and one viewpoint. Not one reporter grasped why the ALP felt so strongly about its governance, none understood the pain and suffering the ALP would endure to enforce its decisions. It was easier for the media assembled at the ALP Annual Conference to characterise the 700 delegates who voted against the Iemma government as captives of unions.

Ignorance of history was wilful. 1916 was as remote as 1066 – though as with Britain and the Conquest, one cannot understand the ALP without understanding 1916. Morris Iemma paid the highest price for appearing to be prepared to ignore the pledge he had signed each time he renewed his ALP membership. The media thought nothing of that key detail. The past did not count for the media. The media savoured Iemma's decision not to attempt to persuade the ALP membership – a necessarily prolonged exercise, largely out of sight, success far from certain. A blitz of editorials and columns was solidly in favour of privatisation and the determination not to countenance opposition by the ALP, a supportive enclosure of words that served only to make delegates teach no end of a lesson. When the media applauded the government's obligation to the electors, these same opinion pieces necessarily were demanding that the government treat with contempt the party to which they held membership obligations.

Unconsidered in the applause bestowed upon Iemma by the media was where that disposition left the ALP or the concept of membership participation, the basis of the McKell model which had served NSW Labor so very well since 1941. The parliamentary gallery listened only to government spinners leavened by the views of Labor MPs who were prepared to vote against the government. Those determined to enforce Conference's will kept their own counsel. John Robertson pulled back as well, so as not to become the issue. One side of the story scored coverage in the media. It was the losing side. The plenitude of errors in the daily papers will fill a textbook on how not to report a story.

The early narrative presumed that Iemma's leadership was in trouble but not because of opposition to electricity. The fantasies piled up. Opposition to privatisation was a feint for those plotting vengeance for Paul Gibson and the ongoing positioning of John Watkins for the succession. Reporters reacted with excitement to any meeting that did not explode, as if the absence of explosion translated into the government prevailing. Throughout the crisis, except for Annual Conference, none of the meetings known to the media was other than tame. Most of the meetings that mattered and most of the phone calls were not known to the media. In those exchanges there were explosions aplenty. The media loved anything that amounted to a tricky manoeuvre such as bypassing Parliament. Later it loved the notion of thumbing a nose at the ALP Conference. When the leadership changed, they had missed the story.

Formalities and ritual

Bernie Riordan delivered the presidential address. Riordan was astute in showering praise extensively, without regard to faction. A sound way to build a speech. Young blokes circulated the Right's journal, *Labor Leader*. Such is the absence of debate inside the ALP and inside the factions that journals appear irregularly, if at all, except for those issues published for the Conference delegates. For the first time ever, there were no attacks on the 'Left'. The two factions had agreed to hold off on the weak point of the other. There would be no mention by the Right of Milton Orkopoulos facing a trial for sexual assault on minors; no mention by the Right's notional opponents of Wollongong's 'Table of Knowledge', a plastic amenity adorning a beach-side kebab shop at which local Right operatives sought to determine the fate of that fine city.

Riordan welcomed new delegates. He invited them to put their name on a speakers' list. 2007 had been a remarkable year. Riordan thanked the people in the back rooms who had worked 14 hours a day for seven days throughout the year as the state election was followed by the federal. He enjoined everyone to behave with courtesy when Iemma addressed them. 'Conference is not a zoo. If you want to boo, hiss, catcall, go outside.' With force he added: 'Some believe this conference is irrelevant. In that case, why have one?' He invited us to turn through the Rule Book. No one was forced to join the ALP. We signed the Pledge. If you don't want to follow the Rules, you don't have to stay. He compared today with the debate of 1997 and the acceptance of that Conference vote as binding.

The role of the rank and file is not only handing out how to votes, Riordan noted. If you do not have the capacity to discuss and promote policy, why be a member? 'It is an important day, a sad day, a day of history, a day of principle and moral fibre', Riordan emphasised. In the space below the galleries – like the much bigger alcoves below the galleries in the Town Hall – there are those who hover and chat.

State MPs filed onto the stage. Not a lot of room, nothing like the long rows behind the stage at the Town Hall designed to house the largest choir. The Premier's address was the second delivered by Morris Iemma. An election victory had intervened. Iemma should have been returning in triumph one year ago, except that the machine had cancelled the 2007 conference for reason of the federal election. The 'annual' in Annual Conference is a furphy: it takes place only as and when it was convenient for the machine to hold it.

The Premier's address

The importance for the leader of an address to Conference cannot be overstated. Even with the aura of Conference gone, much of its authority forfeited to the full-time officials of the party, the speeches by parliamentary leaders provide theatre for an assembly of people who should be the most supportive in the land. Delegates paying attention will weigh the sureness of enunciation, the blendings of gravity and humour, the substance and the quips, the items for the day. Very important is touching base with history, the passages where the leader pays homage to the giants he is following and the giants he is, of course, addressing this day. Neville Wran and Bob Carr were masters of the Conference speech. Between them they spoke to conferences for an uninterrupted span of 28 years. Carr looked upon speechmaking as one of the most satisfying parts of being leader.

Simplicity is a foreign country. A man does not just rise to his feet these days and speak, that is old politics. A pageant of light and sound precedes arrival. Entry is a procession – though that is more difficult in this auditorium. So it was that Morris Iemma arrived with his wife Santina. Most of the male MPs were in suits. Iemma spoke with a sort of choke, a septosyllabic speaking style perhaps induced by shifting his eyes between two autocues.

Applause was muted. Usually it followed a staged pause that invited the joining of hands. Iemma paid tribute to 'a man called John Robertson'. His oratory embraced what the government was delivering on. When the rhetoric claimed rail ran on time, the laughter was embarrassingly loud. The reaction was not malice or disrespect, simply an inability to contain embarrassment at a claim so ridiculous and known to be ridiculous to anyone on a rail line. Such laughter was unprecedented during a leader's speech. The more usual response to a leader's speech is reverent silence, broken by applause. That had been the response to Iemma in 2006. In the meantime he had won an election and lost the support of his party.

By now the seats were mainly occupied. Delegates were paying close attention, waiting for the switch to electricity. It came with mention of a challenge: the new challenge was keeping pace with energy demand. New South Wales must replace power stations, introduce clean product and compete in a national market. New South Wales needs more power, demand will double in the next decade. In 2014 the lights could go out. The time to act is now.

Some boos broke out. Without an increase in supply, business will not invest. Cries of 'Rubbish' were vocal. To build the new plant will cost $15 billion. The money must be spent. Who pays? 'It's not your choice', was one cry. Interjections were flowing freely. The government was pressing against its credit limits. Iemma compared the choices to a family paying off a mortgage. Mocking laughter was the response. Riordan intervened in an attempt to enforce silence. Why divert $15 billion into electricity assets when we could enter private partnerships?

The timing and the atmospherics were wholly wrong. The Premier was addressing a Conference of his party, having made his intentions clear, having floated the possibility that he might proceed whatever the decision. Senior ministers had gone out of their way to offend the sensibilities of the Labor Party. Now the Premier and his ministers were seeking to persuade those they seemed to have insulted gratuitously. This day should have been the beginning of the debate – or the third or fourth year. The Premier should have been according Conference the ultimate respect of announcing his intentions on electricity, acknowledging the difficulties many delegates would be facing, acknowledging the enormity of what the government was asking of the Conference and the party. Because of that enormity, the Premier could have announced he was not rushing the matter, he did not want anyone to feel their views were not going to be heard and respected.

Privatisation is not a sell-out, Iemma argued. He was not going well. Rubbish was the response. More words, more interjections. Riordan again intervened. 'I have been going to enough conferences over 31 years', Iemma said, 'to know this is an uphill battle. If I had wanted the easy way out, I would never have taken this job, I would never have set the bar so high.' His points earned a lukewarm applause. Attempts by cheerleaders to sustain anything beyond the perfunctory were failing.

'It's not easy', admitted Iemma, 'It's not comfortable ...'. 'It's not on', cracked a wag and brought the show down. Iemma appealed for an act of courage. The speech had swayed not a person.

Luke Foley offered a vote of thanks. He mentioned the presence of Neville Wran and Barrie Unsworth, who rose in their places to accept the applause. Foley was generous in paying tribute to Iemma: 'Differences on electricity will not obscure you are Labor and what you have done. The conference desires only the closest association of your government and the party. You honour us with your presence.'

The Premier's address had not gone well. Iemma knew it. The frustration of all those months of negotiations was not always contained. Iemma was not hostile to those who were going to vote against his proposals. He was mindful as he spoke of the attitudes of the members of Beverly Hills Branch. Even with so much on his mind, he was not wanting to offend stalwart members of the party. His hostility was intended for the union leadership who had blocked a decision of any kind. Such subtleties were necessarily lost. The Premier had allowed himself to be portrayed as the enemy of internal party democracy.

Debate on privatisation

The Finance and Economics Committee was the rubric under which the privatisation debate would be taking place. Barrie Unsworth, a redoubtable Conference warrior throughout the 1970s and 1980s, led the debate. Unsworth provided an outline of the reasoning behind his inquiry on behalf of the government. During Unsworth's speech, an amendment in the name of Matt Thistlethwaite (then an official of Unions NSW) was circulated. It was devastating to the government. The language was express. The concluding paragraphs placed beyond doubt the consequences for defying or not heeding the affirmation of 1997:

> Conference notes that the government's proposal is a breach of party policy, and directs State MPs not to support the proposal. Conference further reminds all members of parliament that they have signed a pledge to uphold party policy, as determined by the ALP Conference. Therefore,

members of the State Parliamentary caucus, including all members of cabinet, are reminded that they are bound by the Party Platform and policy as determined by the most recent Annual Conference.

Conference requests that the incoming Administrative Committee contacts all members of the State Parliamentary Labor Party informing them of the Conference decision in relation to privatisation and reminding them of the pledge.

For a government flirting with a repeat of 1916, it had earned for itself an instruction from the party characteristic of 1916.

Unsworth made a lawyer's presentation. The key players were mobile. The extent of the movement was a consequence of geography. At the Town Hall, movement off the stage required a journey to the side and rear to go down stairs onto the floor, then an equally long journey along a narrow corridor back to the body of the hall. The person journeying disappeared for several seconds. In this auditorium going on and off the stage was a matter of two steps. The traveller was always in sight.

Robertson was now in front of the stage. Unsworth was drawing jeers. Riordan had handed the chair to a vice president so he was free to roam. Vice President Michael Williams directed the people under the galleries to sit. They were blocking a fire exit. Ironic cheers. Unsworth was not changing minds. Robertson was moving around. Unsworth kept going. He praised Iemma. He dealt with the Thistlethwaite amendment. Accustomed to winning on the conference floor, he was not relishing what was ahead. 'I am not happy with the prospect of rejection. I do not take kindly to your words, John.'

Kirk McKenzie, by right of being committee chairman, spoke next and supported Unsworth. The situation is complex, Kirk noted, but I can explain it simply. The party has followed policy, the government decides. You cannot direct the executive government. The chair announced the debate ahead was going to embrace four amendments and 28 speakers. The time was already 4:50. Tony

Sheldon provided a distraction by speaking on independent contractors. The managers of the debate did not separate electricity from all other matters.

The amendment standing in the name of Thistlethwaite was instead moved by John Robertson. His speech was a great speech. One of those occasions when the text, the rhetoric, the passion and the audience are as one. He did not muck around with Unsworth. 'John Ducker once told me there's nothing more ex than an ex.' There were those highly critical of Robertson for this swipe. Robertson had decided that Unsworth had forfeited his status once he elected to mix it.

Robertson told stories of call centres where the women were frog-marched out, their jobs relocated to Bangalore. The Competition Commission will not accept a deal on prices: Michael Costa has shown me the letter, Robertson revealed. This morning the Premier spoke of a cost of $15 billion. We should not have to make the choice. The comment was greeted by the loudest applause of the day. We expect more from Labor governments. We look after those who elect us. Loud applause.

Thistlethwaite seconded. Riordan had moved to the far right of the stage. Unsworth's finger was active with Riordan. John Della Bosca looked elsewhere. A reference was made to a new amendment. Costa returned to the stage at 5:08. Usually, even in the most intense factional strife, the principals remain in their seats, runners run whatever messages need running. The difference: this debate was not of faction. The behaviour of the government had given cause for the factions to unite against the government.

Bernie Riordan returned to the floor. He sat on the step next to his father, Joe Riordan, himself a veteran of the union movement, a minister in the Whitlam government. Della Bosca was speaking to Unsworth, who was anchored on the far right of the stage, about the one fixed point on that stage. Costa came onto the stage, to the left of Unsworth. Williams called on people to settle down. Not every speaker was well known. Lorraine Usher of the CFMEU noted that not only unions were opposed. Della Bosca was talking with Costa and Unsworth. Riordan returned and sat on the right of Della Bosca. Some of these people have known each other for three and four decades. Their respective status had altered totally.

Kristina Keneally (Minister for Disability Services) offered a homily that we should be looking out for the disabled and the mentally ill, who will not be looked after because the money won't be there. Jeering reached a crescendo. Williams had to intervene. A low moment for Keneally, a speech that missed entirely the mood of the moment. Riordan took a point of order to plead for decorum. The opponents of the government were terrified of accusations the Conference intimidated the outcome, the precaution was sensible. Riordan could not keep still, like a cat on a hot tin roof. Costa raised his fist. The vote was taking too long to arrive.

Deputy Premier John Watkins felt the need to speak on behalf of the government. Some, Watkins said, had suggested he should not. Conference was a place to debate with vigour. Few dispute the costs of future demands on the state. More invoking of schools, hospitals, roads. Costa was in the ear of the General Secretary, Karl Bitar, who was looking back. Watkins did well enough. He scored some cheers and subdued applause. Impressive in this gathering.

Costa came off the stage. Riordan was out of sight. Della Bosca took the lectern, spoke of his first conference back in 1976 – which proved to be his last for a while because he did not do what his faction wanted. There will always be tensions, he said, between Conference and the Labor Party in government. You've got to understand the tensions. They are not easy to resolve. This dispute had been going on for six or eight months. A lot has happened since 1976. Many enterprises have been sold, most by Labor governments. The sales were because governments came up against inevitable problems. 'If you do not give us permission, understand what you are doing.' Della Bosca was making a significant concession by acknowledging the supremacy of Conference. Everyone knew he was not an economic rationalist, he said, he did not believe in the purity of the market. He repeated the phrase about permission. In three or four budgets time, the money will dry up.

Della Bosca had made a most effective speech. Watkins and Della Bosca were the stars for the government.

Paul Bastian (AMWU) was amazed by how at odds was the proposition for the party. Lease is a weasel word. If it walks like a duck and so on. Paul Gibson MP spoke of the opposition in his electorate. Initially, the sale price was $20 billion, then $15 billion, this morning the Premier said $10 billion. 'If that's not prostituting yourself for a few dollars, I'm a poor judge.' Ministers Reba Meagher and Eric Roozendaal came onto the stage. 'If the Premier goes to the National Executive,' Gibson charged, 'he becomes a lame duck Premier'.

Reba Meagher (Minister for Health) was booed upon being called. She claimed to be a passionate supporter of the trade union movement – except, it seems, when it stands up for itself. In Health the demands are enormous. She was shocked that Robertson (unnamed) thought you could have both no sale and the spending. Meagher did not reach anyone. (Were only ministers going to speak on behalf of the government?) Meagher claimed opposition was more about ego than reason. One wondered what part of Robertson's ego was boosted by taking on this government. Meagher finished with Della Bosca's phrase about permission.

Gerard Martin MP (Bathurst) was opposed. He recalled that Costa sold Freightcorp to Chris Corrigan who had promptly closed down the depot in Lithgow. Why would you have faith in the private sector just now, when world equity markets are reeling? Each of the speakers in opposition to privatisation managed one or more points of their own. The ministers were essentially saying the same – there isn't enough money, demands on the state are huge, we the government have to make a hard decision.

Steve Curren of the Monaro State Electorate Council was one of two non-ministers to speak on behalf of the government. As he set about an attack on Robertson, a chant began of 'Quack, quack, quack'. Grant McBride MP, representing the ETU, thought it was Groundhog Day. He related a visit to the La Trobe Valley in 1997 organised by Ian Macdonald. Macdonald was taking a different position now.

In 1997 on the conference floor this same Ian Macdonald had threatened Michael Egan that the party would come after him if he tried to reintroduce privatisation. In the 11 years since, Macdonald has become 'Della's pet crocodile' – Bob Carr's delicious phrase – and now occupied Egan's portfolio. Macdonald had gone missing. The government was on the ropes, a succession of ministers was speaking outside their portfolios in defence of their government, the Minister for Energy was missing in action. No one was surprised by his absence.

Russ Collison (AWU) devastated the likes of Meagher and Keneally for invoking the disabled and the mentally ill. 'The reference was despicable', said Collison. The powerful voice of a union official who had once worked on off-shore rigs routed the efforts of the ministers. If Robertson had been the surgical director of the case against privatisation, Collison demolished the vestiges of the government's case for. The government had nought going for them on the floor but captives. Whatever overriding loyalty to the government existed before Robertson finished – which was not much given the way it had played the politics – was wholly gone after the collision with Collison.

Eric Roozendaal (Minister for Roads) scored plenty of boos as he came forward. He had attended 22 conferences. This was the first where he did not have the numbers. He wondered if Unions NSW possessed a printing press to print the money the government needed. He proceeded to mock the basic capacity of Labor Party members to understand the economy. Roozendaal invoked support from Kevin Rudd, Martin Ferguson, Unsworth, Carr.

Then it happened. The moment was always going to happen. The fatal words would be spoken – it was always likely Roozendaal would speak them. Someone from the government would step into the shoes of Billy Hughes: 'I was elected not to do what I was told by trade union bosses and delegates. I was elected by the people of New South Wales.' Consider that assertion.

Roozendaal was elected to the Legislative Council because he had a number on the ALP how-to-vote card. He had and has no base in the community. Roozendaal's place on the ticket was the gift of the union bloc vote, as decided by union bosses and delegates. Roozendaal's working life and advancement has been the reward for blind loyalty from union bosses to ALP Head Office and the General Secretary. Roozendaal had no cause for complaint when union bosses selected him for his first job in Head Office and endorsed his rise to General Secretary. Roozendaal had no cause for complaint when union bosses gave him the nod for a winnable spot on the Legislative Council ticket. The creature and creation of union bosses had denounced his creators.

Boos drowned out Roozendaal. The reactions to Keneally, Meagher and Roozendaal were a first for each of them. The mustering of arguments under pressure when the numbers are not assured, when only persuasion will avail, had not been demanded of any of these people during their unstoppable rise to the glittering heights. Not in Young Labor, where they could and did utter nonsense confident it would arouse cheers. Not at previous conferences where they performed for the managers of the Right in order to gain preferment. Not in Caucus nor Cabinet, where debate is limited and their majority is assured. Certainly not in Parliament, which has ceased to be a deliberative forum. This day humbug registered as humbug. Empty rhetoric came over as vacuous. Wild appeals to emotions sounded like hysteria. The faction leaders of the Right were embarrassed by what they had wrought. They had the evidence of their own eyes and ears of what has been wrought by allowing the political class to control candidate selection and dominate preferment for the ministry. Word of how badly his ministers had performed duly reached Iemma, no effort put into softening their collective failure.

Costa and Riordan finish the debate

Michael Costa decided to enter the debate. Iemma believed he had a deal with the machine for a short, sharp debate after which the vote would be taken and the government would know the extent of its defeat. The machine chose not to recognise there was a deal, or chose to break it. Both sides knew how Costa would be feeling after a long debate in which he would be sorely provoked. The machine was counting on a Costa intervention in the certain knowledge that his words and manner would alienate the Conference delegates. Iemma held the same fears. The longer the debate continued, given Costa was present, he could not credibly stay out. Bernie Riordan has refuted this assertion. According to Riordan, Costa was always going to speak. One of their many exchanges on the stage had been Costa's demand to speak last. Riordan stated he (Riordan) would be speaking last. 'I'm the Treasurer', said Costa to Riordan. 'And I'm the party President, I'm speaking last. If you wait', Riordan warned, 'you will miss out'.

Costa's intervention had the effect his friends and detractors had anticipated. He entered the debate, second last to Riordan. The policy of the government, he declared, was Riordan97. Riordan had offered dishonesty after dishonesty. Costa was shouting and, as he shouted, the index finger on his right hand was pointing at Riordan. He switched to a clenched right fist. He banged the lectern with both hands. Riordan wanted to sell retail. The opposition was about ego and power. Across the floor, delegates mocked Costa with their own index fingers. 'Your ego', they shouted back. Costa claimed that Riordan and Robertson were suffering from 'sibling rivalry' – a claim that passed us all by.

'You don't care', Michael yelled. The finger was again pointing. Privatisation will mean more jobs. The Premier won the election. Riordan took to his feet and leaned toward Costa from the corner of the table – but beyond swinging distance – his stance one of rapt attention. From his performance on that weekend, scarcely a soul did not conclude that Costa was other than stark, raving bonkers. The conclusion was wrong and unfair. Michael Costa slams against the confines of his own intellect. When he does, anything can happen. Gifted people have this problem. Indulging them is not the answer.

When Riordan received the call, he virtually jumped out of the box. Williams called the tellers together. He asked the non-delegates to depart. Riordan recited what happened 11 years ago.

He eschewed passion for attention to the economics, a more sensible approach, a blindsiding of Costa. In the matter of dividends, Costa was claiming they were worth $500 million. Add them up and you get $1.4 billion. If the sale is now worth only $10 billion, you need a return of 14 per cent to gain the equal. That will not happen. This year the dividends will grow to $2 billion. Mount Piper will cost $3.1 billion and will last 40 years. What mugs the private sector must be: they were prepared to shell out 25 big ones for what is now worth only 10, a number which itself varied. The packages on sale in both years were never quite certain.

The Bitar–Foley amendment

Hectic activity on the stage was explained when Karl Bitar announced an amendment in his name and Luke Foley's. The amendment was that the government continue to negotiate with unions and other stakeholders. There was no excuse for giving up, said Bitar. Riordan moved around the floor indicating support for this initiative. The cost of going to war was too high, he stated. Foley, seconding the amendment, claimed the support of every union involved in the debate.

The problem for Bitar and Foley was that, unexplained, this amendment sounded like a substitute for the earlier Robertson amendment, an alternative to the harsh, express language of direction. If correct, the two factions were stopping on the edge of the last ditch. A direction to the Caucus was a powerful tool in the coming showdown; an injunction to keep talking amounted to frittering away the opposition that had assembled so solidly on the Conference floor. Foley provided a lesson in history going back to the first Conference of 1892. (Foley had provided much the same in private to the highest levels of the government. Their interest was zero.) That first Conference had asserted its supremacy. The 1894 Conference had inserted the Pledge which remained binding on all MPs. Today's 71 state Labor MPs were the direct heirs of the first Caucus.

Around the auditorium there was serious confusion about the purport of the Bitar–Foley intervention. A great many of the

'Left' delegates thought it was a betrayal. What was perplexing was whether the Bitar amendment substituted for the Robertson amendment. The answer was supplied inadvertently by the Finance Committee chairman, Kirk McKenzie, who was cast as the final speaker. Everyone who mattered wanted him up and down in no time. McKenzie had about 20 seconds – but that was sufficient to achieve nuclear fission. In stating the attitude to the various amendments moved along the way, he offered an *ex parte* that the Robertson amendment did not affect the platform and was not binding. Uproar followed in every row of the auditorium. Foley exploded on stage.

Senator-elect Doug Cameron (representing the Metal Workers' Union) was shouting for a point of order. Often a conference speaker, Cameron had stayed clear of this debate. Part of the consideration in tactics by the 'Left' was that the principal speakers against the government should come from the ruling Right. Now a significant non-Right operative had intervened. Taking a point of order 20 rows back and in the middle was going to be a feat. With uproar reigning, the chair uncertain, Cameron had time to get to the lectern and make his point. He thought the amendment was an amendment to the Platform and was binding. If it wasn't an amendment, then he wanted the opportunity to move an amendment that made it binding. The explanation for these distinctions is that amendments to Platform have to be submitted to Head Office one month in advance of Conference. That had not happened.

This distinction was of no practical importance. Resolutions carried by Conference are binding on party members. In 1979, Conference adopted an urgency motion directing the Wran government not to sell Lotto to private interests – the word 'privatise' was not then part of our lexicon. Neville Wran, without hesitation, put on ice his arrangements with a consortium of Rupert Murdoch and Robert Sangster. Some years ago the General Secretary gained a general authority to increase the number of women in the Legislative Assembly. No one suggested that that resolution was any less binding than a formal amendment to the Platform.

Foley was in a shouting match with someone in a yellow T-shirt – an accident of colour given the shouter was pro-sale. An exchange of blows was not out of the question. The Robertson amendment was going to be put. The critical question was being resolved by the putting of the question: the amendment stood alone and separate to Bitar's. The language of direction was going to survive. The voices were overwhelmingly in favour of the Robertson amendment. Such a question should not be resolved on the voices. Even if only one person supported privatisation, a count was essential to demonstrate to a government determined not to hear how upset were the broad phalanxes of the party. If Michael Egan had insisted on a count in 1997, he could have placed a flag on the field from which the government might have advanced its case. Egan has conceded he was in error in not insisting on a defeat which recorded support for both sides.

> Plenty of egos were on the line over the weekend. And it looks like Iemma and Costa have won the first round.
> (Andrew Clennell, *SMH*, 5 May 2008)

In a democracy it is always better to settle matters by voting. Taking a count settles for the moment how matters stand. Either side can revisit their position provided both sides accept as binding the decision already taken. The modern predilection for settling matters behind closed doors, as if every issue is resolvable by compromise and nuance, has not served Labor well. The push for selling electricity assets might have been achieved by now, or part-achieved, if the government had continued to confront the party. Politics usually follows that sort of logic. There were many who could have entertained a proposition for sale or part-sale. They would not entertain the assertion that the government could arrogate the decision to itself.

The count took a very long time to get started. Television cameras wandered freely, taking in the forest of hands in favour of Robertson. Judging by the few hands against, it seemed unlikely the nays would achieve 100. The count revealed that the only bloc against was the State Parliamentary Caucus, augmented by the delegates from a scattering of electorate councils. MPs stood in their places with cards aloft, enjoying their show. The time was 7:10.

Triumphalism was absent from the forces that had won. They wanted accurate numbers before dispersing. The numbers were devastating: for Robertson 702, against 107. The hubbub in the foyer was one of relief. Delegates dispersed quickly to attend their factional dinners.

Sunday, the morning after

Entering the Convention Centre on the Sunday required production of one's membership card. Security was much stricter. Was this related to the visit by the Prime Minister? It certainly was, said the assertive young security fellow. So if you possessed an ALP membership card, you are less likely to fire a bullet at the Prime Minister? Inside people were milling in the foyers. The Canberra press gallery had arrived in numbers because Rudd was speaking. The story that would last beyond the weekend was yesterday. One reporter trying to understand was Quentin Dempster of the ABC. In a conversation he explained his understanding that Michael Costa achieved amendments to the State Corporations Act that enabled the government to sell assets with the signatures of two ministers. A manoeuvre like that would be dishonourable. It did seem most unlikely, not when one knew how much time and resources of the Parliamentary Counsel were being expended on drafting several pieces of inter-related, interlocking bills on selling electricity. More definite news was that Morris Iemma had convened a press conference for 2:30 this day at the Governor Macquarie Tower, his turf.

One day on, John Robertson was plaintive. Yesterday was not feeling like victory to him. Mark Arbib was in sight for the first time. Robertson had legal advice that Costa could not sell with two signatures. Some had been thinking about a government appeal to the ALP National Executive on the grounds that the proposed legislation conforms with national policy. The National Executive is not an undistracted gathering of law lords on the Privy Council. The National Executive is 21 supremely political operators. Out of 21 members, the 'Left' had nine. That is a long way toward achieving a majority. The additional two votes needed to block the appeal were readily available, beginning with the three Right delegates from New South Wales who would vote against an appeal. Operatives from the other states would not lightly vote against the authority of a State Conference.

For the National Executive to uphold an appeal against a proper decision in New South Wales amounts to destroying party authority. The National Executive is itself an instrument of authority, an authority built and extended since its creation in 1915 by way of asserting that authority over state branches and parliamentary parties. The National Executive will always back authority against rebellion. Without respect for authority in the party, the party will be suspending the laws of gravity. In the absence of the numbers to overrule, the Executive would make no decision. No decision amounted to upholding the decision of Conference.

The auditorium filled for Kevin Rudd. His entry was a long time in coming. When, finally, we were asked to make welcome the Prime Minister, it was another minute or so before he entered the space – though the delegates clapped all the while. Riordan offered an exceptionally long introduction. This Conference was of a mood to forgive Riordan anything. Rudd spoke with the confidence you would expect. Rudd is not an orator, he is certainly not a conference orator. He made light of the difficulties of yesterday. Word came that Iemma had told the media he was proceeding anyway. Yesterday was going to be the easiest day in the lives of Robertson and Riordan for a good while to come. Iemma could not just fold. The struggle moved to Caucus.

If the Caucus opposition grew significantly, resolution came down to what advice the government followed about the appropriate means of achieving a sale. Legislation would bring into play the disposition of the Liberal and National Party Opposition. Their duty was to destroy the government. The views of Nick

Greiner (who had advocated support for the sale) or the merits of sale would be secondary to the strategic imperative of inflicting maximum harm on the government. Barry O'Farrell made that clear in the days following.

Iemma stood up at the press conference while his party was in its Annual Conference. All the night before his phone had run hot. Stories had come to him of MPs, supporters of the sale through six Caucus meetings, now prepared to buckle because of direct threats from machine operatives. Each would-be buckler was rewrapped. None of these MPs had delivered a vote at Conference for reason they lacked support in their own electorates: they were susceptible to threats from those who had made their parliamentary careers possible. Iemma was careful with his language. He was conscious his reaction would cause anger back at the Conference. In trying to be respectful, Iemma laboured one point: if the party does not come with me, the government will take a decision. Those words amounted to defiance if the government could not prevail, words that set up the end-game.

Conference calls the government to account

In the Industrial Relations Committee report, Robertson advised he was aware that the Premier had spoken about the Conference decision. Robertson repeated that Conference decisions were not to be taken lightly. Decisions at Conference were the expression of the will of the trade union movement and the energies of the branches. We should be celebrating victories. It comes down to respect, how we are dealt with. Respect is a commodity in short supply for Michael Costa. Like marriages and other partnerships, parties work because of honesty, mutual support, standing up for each other. Processes are in place to protect this party from attack.

Following a perfectly safe report on industrial relations, the Agenda Committee recommended an urgency motion. The faction leaderships were back in their seats. A crowded stage makes such a difference. Riordan moved the urgency motion: it called for a meeting of the Campaign Committee, a report back to the Administrative Committee, it reaffirmed yesterday's decision – more discussions but inside compliance with Platform and Policy. Riordan noted that no one doubted the need for reform in the electricity industry. The unions have presented seven or eight options to the government. All were rejected out of hand and without reasons, Riordan claimed.

In the closed world of ALP factional manoeuvring, it is likely that people in the same room will have wholly different accounts of what was said and what was agreed to. The total breakdown in trust meant that both sides were accusing the other of not being fair dinkum about a compromise. Riordan welcomed the Premier's comment that they would talk. The unions did not know what the position was. Friday's *Daily Telegraph* had presented a plan totally different to Thursday's discussions. Every aspect of the Costa proposals was bad. 'The performance of Michael Costa was either a deliberate attempt to make the ALP Conference look like a rabble', Riordan said, 'or he needs to go back to see his doctor'.

Luke Foley warned that the party was on the edge of a precipice. All party officers tried to avoid the confrontations. The Premier had laid down a gauntlet to the Labor Party. Della Bosca intervened with a deft performance. Don't be too anxious about what emerged from the media. The Premier does understand what happened. It is not about a word on the page. Della Bosca was happy to mandate that discussions would continue. The Labor Party will get a solution. Paul Bastian (AMWU) spoke before Riordan replied: 'It comes down to this step right now. The MPs are members of the Australian Labor Party, not one would have been elected but for the ALP beneath their name.'

On the voices, one person voted no.

Conference was over at 5:25. The media were overdosing on the story as story. Every commentator and editorial lined up behind the government. The editorials of May 2008 have appeared many times – throughout the 1890s, throughout 1916–17, through the

1950s split, stridently in 1963 and with renewed vengeance in the early Whitlam era. In every era, the mainstream media have encouraged Labor's parliamentary leaders to defy instruction from Labor conferences. In every era, the media have assailed union influence and the rights of unions to act in support of their members. The media do not accept the legitimacy of Labor's governance, though its workings have served this state and nation well for 117 years.

On 6 October 1890, the *Sydney Morning Herald* had warned against the formation of a labour party. As the first Labor Conference of 1892 prepared to meet, the *Herald* denounced the assembly as that of:

> a party that had openly set before itself a politically immoral object – the sacrifice of the general interests to the claims of one class, and that had openly proposed the attainment of that object by an openly immoral method – the offer of its solid vote to the highest bidder.

In the 1890s and through the early years of Federation, the governance of Labor was said to be an affront to the Constitution, the British way of sorting out differences. MPs ceding their consciences to the dictates of Caucus was an act of violence against the Westminster system. To cede final authority to the party that selected you was abdicating to seditious forces. Hostility to the ALP's way of governing itself has been a constant of the media for as long as the party has been a threat to accustomed ways. Hostility to the ALP's way of governing itself has also been a constant for those Labor governments facing the consequences of their own failure to persuade.

There could now be not the slightest doubt that any measure that required approval by both Houses of Parliament would pass only if the Opposition forfeited their best opportunity in 67 years to change the compass of New South Wales politics. If the Opposition fulfilled their constitutional obligation to oppose, legislation which was not approved by the Australian Labor Party was not going to pass into law.

Chapter 5
Morris Iemma falls

All that mattered after the Conference happened off camera. The media had lost interest in the story once it ceased to be the pyrotechnics of abuse. The story revived from time to time when it suited the government to outline its present thinking or that part of such thinking it thought useful to put into the public domain. The actual story, the ongoing story before and after the Conference, required a knowledge of ALP history and tradition – the nuances behind ALP governance that makes a dysfunctional 19th-century party electable and relevant.

The government defies Conference
Once Conference adjourned, most of the delegates scattered to the four winds. They resumed their usual lives. Unlike the political class, they had real jobs with real employers where a real performance was required to earn their wages and salaries. Prosecuting the will of Conference fell to the leadership of Unions NSW and the ALP full-time officers. Omitted from the negotiating table were the representatives of the membership. Omitted were the people who had turned defeat for the government into a rout. The advocates of

Conference supremacy around the table were plagued, some less than others, with doubts about pushing opposition all the way – wherever that might end.

> A mortal blow has been dealt to the union campaign against the State Government's power privatisation plans, with two former union leaders now backing the $10 billion sale and Premier Morris Iemma's decision to defy the party.
>
> (Simon Benson, *Daily Telegraph*, 6 May 2008)

The New South Wales Parliamentary Labor Party met in the week following Conference. That meeting came and went without incident. The media wrote it up as a mighty triumph for Morris Iemma. They did not know that Luke Foley and Eddie Obeid MLC had agreed in advance that it served no one's interest to be testing Caucus numbers in the immediate aftermath of Conference. The Premier would certainly win a test vote, so why risk more MPs peeling off or more MPs being corralled? Note the principals here: Foley, the machine leader of the non-Right minority forces, was speaking for the Conference majority; Obeid was speaking for a government in which he held no office. Iemma fulfilled the terms of the Conference resolution calling for an urgent meeting with the Premier: on the Wednesday he met with Robertson, Riordan and a representative of the 'Left'. Out of that meeting emerged a new process to achieve an outcome.

The Greens in the Legislative Council seized the opportunities for mischief, or worse, by tempting Labor MLCs to support a bill that legislated against any attempt to sell, lease or otherwise dispose of any part of the electricity industry. Labor backbenchers Ian West and Lynda Voltz spoke in support, very briefly, minus rhetoric. Both indicated they would vote in support of the Greens' bill. Both were punctilious in stating their votes were in accordance with a decision of the ALP Conference. They did not consider that they were crossing the floor. When the time came, they had good reason to believe that they would not be alone.

With caucus backing Morris Iemma at yesterday's post-conference meeting, their [the unions'] conference floor victory has now been turned into a complete emasculation.

(Simon Benson, *Daily Telegraph*, 7 May 2008)

The government was not dissuaded by the prospect of defeat in Parliament. Costa believed that the vast majority of Labor MPs were going to stick and the Opposition could not, in the final ditch, vote contrary to basic Liberal Party ideology. By proceeding, the government was daring the ALP (that is, the authority of the Administrative Committee) to exact the sanctions undoubtedly available to the party. Doubt confronted certainty. When doubt plays certainty, usually you can back certainty. Certainty reinforces itself; doubt corrodes. The unfolding language of public confrontation was a discourse between enemy camps. The government was declaring its independence from the ALP. By any fair reckoning, that independence had come to pass. Unless the ALP exacted the price of directing the government – resolved by solemn authority of a Conference resolution – and proceeded to discipline those who defied the direction. The government calculated that the party had not the fortitude to cast members of a Labor government outside the fold.

The Right MPs on the backbenches were not responding to pressures from the machine that had put them there. Not even those without a base in their electorates. They were sticking with the government against their creators. A promise of a ministry, the fear of upsetting one's place in the queue for any ministry, lack of imagination, congenital weakness of character, pandering to the leadership of the government – each of these were factors in the solidarity within Caucus. It was a sign of weakness, not strength. Time would reveal that fear was decisive in causing Caucus to stick with the Premier as, surely, a greater fear later caused Caucus to abandon him.

For daring to point out the wider consequences of defiance, John Della Bosca copped a hammering, with whispers that he had been talking compromise in order to position himself for the succession. Della Bosca had done too well by half at Conference. The whispering took visual form with a posting on YouTube, a redubbing of *Downfall*'s Hitler in the Fuhrerbunker in the last days of the Third Reich – Della Bosca raging that the coup against Iemma has not come to pass. Pro-Della or anti-Iemma forces responded with a dubbing of the same footage, Iemma as Hitler denouncing all those who had opposed the electricity sale. All this handiwork was by persons well-placed and senior within the ranks of ministerial staff. Your tax dollars at work.

> Morris Iemma won an important victory in his bid to privatise the power industry when Labor MPs decided not to take him on in caucus.
>
> (Andrew Clennell, *SMH*, 7 May 2008)

On the parliamentary 'Left', courage was conspicuously lacking. The forthcoming test was not going to be a faction meeting where rhetoric is all the go. Caucus itself was not the test either. It was not sufficient to strut your stuff, mouth the clichés, speak the code expected, vote privately against the government, then fall in meekly as if everything you said did not really matter. The days of a Left-wing cell operating within the government, proudly apart on matters of non-negotiable principle, are long over. The ultimate vote on electricity, the only vote that mattered, was going to take place in the broad daylight of the floor of the two Houses. What would matter was the column in *Hansard* where the names appeared. Posturing ahead of that moment counted for nought.

The choice was a novelty – a vote against Caucus and for Conference. When the rhetoric was done and dusted, when the declarations of firm intent were made, the actual and certain votes against the government – misleadingly described as 'crossing the floor' – were a handful in the Legislative Council and no one for absolute certain in the Assembly. If five Labor MLCs truly did vote against the government, the legislation would pass only if the Opposition voted for it.

New South Wales politics had joined Alice on the other side of the looking glass. The union movement and the Australian Labor Party were depending on the Liberal and National Parties to defend them from the legislative ambitions of a Labor government. The Opposition was experiencing its own difficulties. Their course should have been self-evident: fulfil the constitutional obligation to oppose the government. Take whatever steps are necessary to bring down the government or, if that is not immediately possible, hasten that outcome. The Coalition's role in politics is not to meet the policy agendas of Fairfax or News Limited. NSW Labor has not done too badly for most of its history in offending those sensibilities.

The formula for voting against the legislation was easily recited: 'The Opposition supports privatisation but not this package of measures. The Opposition does not trust this government to implement privatisation.' Given the eagerness with which the government sought to accommodate the conditions of Her Majesty's Opposition, its ongoing gambit would surely be to introduce newer and more stringent conditions. The Opposition needed to test to the full the determination of Michael Costa. Move incrementally the scale of concessions, meanwhile revealing the depths of the government's desperation until, finally, the government drew a line in the sand – if they drew a line in the sand. The concessions would make the choice of voting against the government so much easier for those who were thus far without conscience in dishonouring the ALP Pledge. It was hard to see how the government could win, or how the Opposition could lose, provided the Opposition remembered their role in politics.

The unions had taken on the MPs at Conference, showed them what for, booed them for their arrogance. Having voted with the representatives of the ALP membership to crush the MPs, union leaders found that, incredibly, the MPs were bent on ignoring the Conference. Much muttering took place and cogitations more sober of a day of reckoning for those who owed the unions everything. The Premier gave notice in mid-May that he was introducing the enabling legislation for privatisation. The notice coincided with a delegates' meeting of electricity unions who resolved to campaign against the legislation and campaign against those Labor MPs who voted for it. We would see.

Was there not a greater danger that John Robertson was going to be cut down in the grounds of the palace by his rivals within the unions? Had Morris Iemma not achieved a permanent redefining of power within state Labor? The parliamentary Labor Parties, state and federal, have become the only prizes worth having. In the fullness, both Bernie Riordan and John Robertson expected to go into parliament. Were they prepared to take whatever action was required to smash the pretensions of Caucus-as-spaceship when their own futures would be on board these galactic vehicles? Does anyone any longer envisage a career in the party administration? Does anyone hope to spend the remainder of their days in the service of union members? Unions and the machine they created have become a host body for birds of passage with a radar homed on a house of parliament before their 35th birthday.

With all the parties so aligned, a coalition of concerned forces proceeded to avoid the test of a vote on the floor of either House of Parliament. If they could bring down the Iemma leadership and force out Michael Costa, a new leadership would not proceed with the privatisation. Changing the leader of NSW Labor was not going to be a walk in the park. Extraordinary events would have to intervene – over and above the giddy unlikeliness of all that had happened already.

The ruling Right had not provided an alternative leader should Morris Iemma fall. John Della Bosca was in the wrong chamber and found himself in trouble on several fronts. The ideological withering of what called itself the ALP Left provided the benefit that its adherents came with no baggage. Of the 2007 intake,

Nathan Rees and Verity Firth were the standouts. Carmel Tebbutt had stood aside after the election to devote time to her child – a decision which provided her with increased media interest, not less. Her return remained a matter for speculation in bad times and worse, which was essentially every waking moment of the then government from the day it announced its Cabinet after the 2007 election.

> The campaign to dump Morris Iemma is dead in the water. Fini. Kaput. Terminado. Or, as they would say in Eskimo, innerpok!...the plot is officially foiled.
>
> (Simon Benson, *Daily Telegraph*, 30 July 2008)

Labor hardheads well knew that the government could not rely on a quasi-forfeit as in 2007. Private polling traced the extent of Iemma's decline. The decline was steep. Bitar decided it was irreversible. Very early on, surveying the talent available, Bitar and his Assistant General Secretary, Luke Foley, decided to make Nathan Rees leader. Independently they had come to that view and joined forces. Poor polling was the only reason that Bitar gave Foley for the future move against Iemma. Mark Arbib was a part of their thinking, agreed with it but, given he had left Head Office and was hoping to play a role in the Rudd government, he decided to play no direct role. He would always be there, well out of sight. Arbib is a master of remaining out of sight.

The emergence of Nathan Rees

Foley had come to know Rees not through the activity of faction but through his work for Bob Carr. The party had held strategy sessions with the Carr government: Arbib, Bitar and Foley met with Carr's senior staff – Walt Secord, Amanda Lampe and Graeme Wedderburn. Carr was aloof to that. Sometimes Rees was dragged in. Rees impressed everyone. People of goodwill marked him for a higher purpose. Morris Iemma was an enthusiastic supporter of getting Rees into Parliament.

Nathan Rees was born in Sydney in 1968, the older of two children of Darryl and Frances Rees. He grew up in Sydney's west, the son of a school teacher father and a mother who was a legendary activist within the ALP and its then Left. Nathan attended Epping Heights Public School, then Northmead High where he obtained his HSC. He was an outstanding athlete and lover of sports. But for an accident, his cycling might have taken him to the Olympics. Deliberately, he avoided entering university in favour of seeking trade qualifications as a greenkeeper while working for Parramatta City Council. It was while watering a strip of grass, pondering where he might be in 30 years, that he decided he did not want to be watering grass. Rees undertook an Arts degree which resulted in Honours in English with the result he was well read and on top of new literature. He loved poetry and much preferred the scripts of plays to a performance in the theatre. At an ALP fund-raiser in Murrumbateman during his premiership he dazzled the audience with a word perfect rendering of a passage from Scott Fitzgerald's *The Great Gatsby*, without notes, in response to the speech introducing him.

After a period as a clerk in the Commonwealth Public Service, Rees returned to Sydney in December 1997 to commence employment in the ranks of the ministerial staff of the Carr government. Over the next 10 years he worked for Andrew Refshauge, Craig Knowles, Iemma and Carr. A lot of ministers were vocal in their support for his entry to Parliament. The opening came with the decision to remove a defector from 'Left' to Right from her safe seat where Rees lived and had the numbers. She resisted to no avail. In the complexities of Sydney in and around Parramatta, two safe seats were becoming available. Laurie Ferguson, the federal member for Reid, sought to control events. One element was a trade-off for vacant seats coming into play in and around Newcastle. A deal was done. It excluded Rees. The deal was undone because Morris Iemma intervened. Rees' candidacy was supported by Iemma, John Watkins and Bitar. Six seats – Newcastle, Toongabbie, Granville, Drummoyne, Shellharbour and Parramatta – went to the National

Executive, which installed those Iemma favoured. Local membership of the Labor Party played no role in these selections. The exercise of the plenary powers by the National Executive was ludicrous. It was another step in the killing of the Labor Party below, made possible because the Labor Party branches in those electorates were already so weak. Upon election in 2007, Rees immediately became a minister. He was again supported by Iemma and Watkins.

> The assumption that Iemma would roll over – if not immediately on being shown mysterious internal polling that everyone now admits doesn't exist, then following a sustained backroom assault – was badly miscalculated. They forgot to put a usurper in the castle.
>
> (Simon Benson, *Daily Telegraph*, 30 July 2008)

The first Bitar–Foley plan did not envisage Rees as Premier, though he did have the potential to be deputy. Arbib and Bitar had been and were essential to Iemma's premiership. For Bitar now to move against Iemma was like moving against family. The plot was not cold-blooded, nor ruthless. No one felt pleasure in what they had to do. The long passages where little appeared to be happening were the pauses that occur when players at loggerheads seek to preserve honour all round. Bitar had research conducted during autumn 2008, February through March, at the same time as the machine was working toward a settlement on electricity ahead of Annual Conference. The findings were far worse than what was feared. Not a detail leaked. The polling convinced the machine that Iemma's leadership would take the party to annihilation. Worse was the group associated with Iemma – Michael Costa, Reba Meagher, Frank Sartor, Joe Tripodi. The only option was a cleanskin. Only two names fitted the bill – Nathan Rees and Carmel Tebbutt.

Falling out between Premier and machine

Iemma was well aware that he had lost the confidence of the party machine. Even though Arbib had asked him to stand for the leadership, Iemma was not the Premier that the General Secretary had been expecting. Arbib trespassed into matters of policy detail not ordinarily of concern to a party official. Like a master lecturing a pupil, oblivious to the change in status that the premiership confers on even the closest of friends, Arbib was relentless in his criticisms of Iemma. Arbib did not let up on Iemma's style, his policies, the make-up of the Cabinet, especially at forums where the party sat down with the government's leadership. According to Iemma, one example that grated with him was Arbib's demand that the government announce mandatory sentencing because the polling supported that announcement. Arbib also had intelligence that Debnam would make such an announcement. Iemma refused point-blank. By refusing to enter the customary race to the bottom on law and order that generally characterises New South Wales elections, Iemma achieved a critical differentiation with the Coalition parties.

Desalination of the ocean's water was an issue of major internal contention. The government intended to commit to a desalination plant. The ALP office said no. The party officers were ringing ministers directly. Iemma could recall nothing like the scale of this interference when he had entered the Cabinet in 1999. Certainly such interventions by the machine were unknown in the Wran and Unsworth eras. The premier of the day, as leader of the parliamentary party, did expect the machine to express its views forcefully if it thought decisions made or decisions pending were having an electoral impact that Cabinet had not expected. The interventions in the Iemma period were of a scale that indicated Arbib, as General Secretary, had developed a sense of entitlement to influence decisions. Going into the 2007 election, the tensions between the leader and the machine were electoral, political and personal. They were acute and, as it proved, irredeemable.

For none of these activities does Arbib make an apology. The party machine is entitled to express its views forcefully. For the most part, the machine was pressing for decisions, any decision, to get issues off the canvas. Part of the general secretary's job is to pursue donations from all lawful sources. Like all previous secretaries, Arbib was assiduous in pursuing developers, publicans and the Jewish community. He expected the Premier, ministers and MPs to attend fundraisers to help fill campaign coffers. Some of these people Iemma refused to see. (On fraternising with developers, Iemma was more punctilious than most party leaders.) At the time the machine was waging an open campaign to destabilise Sartor. Karl Bitar was vicious about Sartor, criticisms couched in terms of the need to get things moving. Sometimes Iemma told developers to go to blazes (the words employed were less polite).

Luke Foley was astonished by the freedom with which Arbib and Bitar presumed to ring the Premier, a presumption which no one had dared with Bob Carr. On matters large and small, Arbib and Bitar presumed the right to state to Iemma what they thought were problems and what they thought were solutions. In the recall of Arbib, there were more calls received from the Premier than calls made. Issues like the Cross City Tunnel, a symbol of a government which had abandoned its base, had sunk the government in Labor's strongholds in western Sydney. A decision on water – for or against desalination, for or against recycling – was critical as long as a decision was made. Iemma is no less adamant that Arbib's concern was decisions made he did not like.

The head of any premier is crowded with problems. The essence of good statecraft is preserving space inside a leader's head for creative thinking. The more crowded a leader's head with detail, the less likely he or she will make good decisions. Providing some measure of freedom for thinking time is why a good staff will limit access to a leader. The mobile phone has played no small role in closing down the spaces into which a leader can escape the preoccupations of the moment. Time sorts out the trivial. Immediacy exaggerates the importance of the passing.

In late 2007, Arbib resigned his party office ahead of taking his seat in the Senate in July 2008. Karl Bitar enjoyed a smooth succession. Bitar was very much an Arbib loyalist. Bitar assumed the same sense of entitlement as he had witnessed Arbib assert. This author believes complaints grew that Iemma was not consulting the machine enough, including even the Budget. This was taking a sense of entitlement into wholly new spheres. Iemma was confronting a general secretary with decided views about the extent of his role. Bitar's campaign against the administration of the Health portfolio was relentless. Iemma's manoeuvres on electricity had placed Bitar under a lot of pressure to call a special party conference. Already anxious about the next state election, Bitar had formed the view by 2008 that it was time for a change of leadership. The world would be easier if Iemma and Costa and other difficulties went away.

At a meeting in early 2008, Bitar introduced this most delicate of matters by asking what Iemma was hoping to do. Iemma began an answer on the government's program, only to be interrupted with the observation that polling revealed there were problems for the government. In terms always courteous, Bitar did not spare his friend from his views: the problem is you, there is no way back, it will be better if you depart. Bitar added a list of ministers whose positions were untenable. The published polls were turning as well.

Iemma had always spoken to Arbib and Bitar in acknowledgement that the machine had put him into the leadership. The machine took the view that Iemma regarded himself as the servant of the party. The machine looked upon Iemma's growing hostility as paranoia. Iemma, of course, thought his state of mind was an appropriate response to an unfolding conspiracy. Bitar believed that Iemma would depart voluntarily.

After the Conference in May, Iemma noted that Bitar had redoubled his efforts to get rid of himself, Costa and others. Bitar had by then shared the research findings on Iemma's standing with Arbib and Foley. It does not appear that the machine considered that it might have a responsibility to assist the leader through troubled times, as the machine had done with Carr in 1989 and 1990 and again in 1994. (Learned workshops had once studied how to elect Carr, given the problem of a head that had the wrong shape and a bookish persona. Aficionados had decided Carr was unelectable.)

You did not need polling to know that the electorate was in no mood to forgive Labor after its begrudging endorsement in 2007. A political class in love with the process of politics yielded too few people who could plan, supervise or manage the basic services of government. In a handful of portfolios were ministers unequal to the task. New South Wales was paying a heavy price for the disappearance of the Labor Party below. Iemma did not have the choice of personnel to put into Cabinet that Carr had enjoyed. The impression indelible for the electorate was that the government, when it was not preoccupied by electricity, was not doing anything beyond offering yet more promises about the never-never.

Succession settled

The succession was settled if nought else. Iemma agreed that Rees was the best option. The strategy Nathan Rees was pursuing was impressive. He had nothing to gain and everything to lose by making any move in the cause of his own advancement. The machine was united in elevating him. Even the person facing displacement had sufficient personal regard for Rees to know that he was the only possible replacement. Iemma could have spiked Rees in all sorts of ways. He did not. Nor did he consider it. The chemistry between the then Premier and his certain successor – if (that is) the Premier should be replaced – was possibly unique in Australian politics. Not often do we see a managed succession. Not before have we seen a benign acceptance of a replacement when the incumbent still did not accept that his departure was required.

> It became clear yesterday that the campaign by head office to dump Mr Iemma had been abandoned.
> (Simon Benson, *Daily Telegraph*, 8 Aug 2008)

How does one cope with the knowledge that one will likely become premier? Rees kept to himself. He was elected to Parliament with a swagger intrinsic to his true self, supremely self-confident, a persona at polar opposite to Morris Iemma. Rees did not have to change his manner so as to appear foreman material. Rees is by nature a leader. To the machine he made it clear he would not lift a finger against Iemma. He would stand for a vacancy in the leadership; he would not take action to bring about a vacancy in the leadership.

The public drama was about electricity. Bitar foresaw an all-out war of six to twelve months within the ALP to resist a course set by the government for a sale that was always unpopular with the electorate. Bitar was not able to reach Iemma's inner mind. A friendship had ended, both men realised, though they would have to go on working together. The General Secretary had known the Premier so well, known him before Parliament, known him in Parliament, known him in the Cabinet. What Bitar thought he knew was a political animal – not a criticism or shortcoming. Iemma was now driven by ideology, one identical to that driving Michael Costa. After re-election Bitar thought that Iemma lost his compass points. The machine monitored Iemma's ongoing efforts to get his way on electricity by winning over opponents. The failure on electricity became a secondary reason for Iemma's removal. Iemma could not avoid removal but he was definitely not departing before electricity was resolved, whatever the resolution. Iemma was not prepared to cut and run.

> The campaign to dump Premier Morris Iemma has been officially ended by his own MPs, with a declaration of support for him after a caucus delegation to the leader's office.
>
> (Simon Benson, *Daily Telegraph*, 9 Aug 2008)

The machine leadership prefers to avoid open conflict. The ambition of modern Labor governance is to take conflict off the floor of a conference and all other reportable occasions. The machine was conscious that the McKell model was in grave jeopardy. Bitar may not think in such terms; Foley certainly did. His knowledge of Labor history inclined him to remind Morris Iemma of 1916 and other moments in Labor's past. Iemma believed he was doing everything possible to accommodate the unions. His opponents had promised not a week of clear air once he persisted with the sale of electricity. They had made good that promise. Iemma had been proceeding through early 2008 in the knowledge that the machine already wanted him gone. His proposals on electricity had been routed at Conference. Frustration at any lack of progress became mixed with exasperation that, as Iemma saw it, a handful of individuals in the Caucus and the machine had been undermining him without relent.

Appearances were everything. Iemma appeared to believe the puff of the media, a puff aided and abetted by the wilfulness of his staff in assuring him that he was bigger than the Labor Party that had created him. Iemma has rejected that he ever was taken in by media applause. The demands of the tabloids and 30 seconds on television denied him subtlety. However wrong that perception – and Morris Iemma credibly insists it is totally wrong – the perception harmed the Premier's standing among the party membership, especially that coterie which sought and gained election as delegates to Annual Conference.

No compromise possible

Bitar and Foley were men on a mission on two fronts: enforce the sovereignty of Conference; bring down a premier acting in defiance of his party, plus whomever else was necessary. As the most senior officers in the ALP, they were seeking to ensure that the Rules of the ALP were followed. It would have been extraordinary if they had taken any other course.

Iemma intended to prevail over the Labor Party he led. He had lost confidence in its processes. He was entitled not to have any confidence in a Conference so unrepresentative of the modern electorate and the broad mass of Labor voters. He was not entitled to defy its decisions, not when he had been gifted so much by the faction whose power flowed from a conference so constituted. Not when he had relied on the authority of the conference and its authority for the imposing of his will in earlier times. Iemma has denied that he ever said that he intended to defy conference, though he concedes that that perception had taken hold. He was flirting with expulsion when the government gave notice in Parliament of the electricity bills, an action in express defiance of what Annual Conference had resolved.

The most serious accusation against Iemma is that he was defying the party Pledge. How could he square signing the Pledge with proceeding with the electricity bills after rejection of his proposals by Conference? The accusation of disloyalty is one that properly troubles him. Morris Iemma regarded himself then and always as a party loyalist. The pursuit of electricity privatisation was not wilful, there was none of the brinksmanship characteristic of the conscription crisis of 1916. Iemma did keep going the extra mile to bring his party on-side. He is also entitled to note the willingness of the ALP to permit the privatising of prisons and lotteries without a murmur after he had fallen. The notion that he was vain or egotistical does not accord with knowledge of how he conducted himself when Premier. At no stage, he has noted, did he ever attempt to whip the sale through.

His position could have been wholly different if he had denounced the Conference as unrepresentative and appealed to the membership to join him in a campaign for reform. The sliver of trade unions affiliated to the ALP is increasing its power within the party, an increase inverse to institutional decline and social irrelevance. Iemma did some reaching out – a roadshow in the Hunter, a letter to the membership, visits to the Illawarra and his home turf of St George which doubled as meetings with branches and electorate councils. Iemma was putting his case on electricity without widening the war to one about an unrepresentative party. To denounce the party's structure was going to be an outcome no less terminal for Iemma. In such a defeat he would have enjoyed a phalanx of support and emerged as a martyr for the cause of party democracy. Instead, he was going to perish as the man who sought to override party democracy. The union officials were able to portray themselves as the defenders of what there was left of democracy in the party, even if the absence of democracy was the reason these union officials enjoyed the influence they wielded. Internal party democracy spelled political death for affiliated unions.

Putting the plot together

Removing a premier was territory unknown to all. You had to go back to 1916 to read of the only other deposing. The plotters were aware of the enormity of the task, its gravity and the certainty of consequences beyond prediction. Bringing down Iemma was a long game. The early moves post-Conference were not important. Expulsion was not out of the question. It was one option if the opponents of sale decided that bringing in the National Executive served a purpose. The thinking was that the Executive would take a compromise: lift the expulsion but direct the government to obey Conference. That ploy had to wait.

A story was later fed to Paul Kelly that Kevin Rudd had pleaded with Iemma not to introduce the privatisation ahead of the federal poll. In exchange, Rudd would come out in support when Iemma was ready. Observation one: Iemma had won an unlikely election without a mention of an electricity sell-off. As the sale was unpopular with the electorate, neither the electorate nor the Labor Party had any cause to believe sale was a revivable prospect. Any statements sounded like sale was off the agenda. There was serious alarm in the machine at the prospect that Iemma might make the official response to the Owen Inquiry in the midst of APEC, an international conference held in Sydney and dominating headlines in mid-2007. The Owen report amounted to a green light for sale. Iemma has denied he ever had such intentions. A federal election was imminent. Bitar went to the Premier's office in the Governor Macquarie Tower where he camped until he was given the moment to say what he needed to say. It was not a plea but an instruction: in his capacity as state campaign director, Bitar dictated that the government could not respond to that report until the federal election was out of the way. Iemma has denied the government intended to act during APEC or ahead of the federal election.

In April 2008, just ahead of the Conference, Rudd received plain talking from wise owls that he would be extremely unwise to intervene in New South Wales. Rudd was told in unambiguous terms that his intervention would cut no mustard on the National Executive. Rudd was given to understand that Cabinet solidarity did not apply in internal party affairs. Ministers would openly defy their Prime Minister. A majority on the National Executive was locked in. The NSW Right outside the Parliament had held solid. Right MPs had not shifted their local branches opposed to privatisation; their impact was zero in their own electorate councils. Not a single trade union broke from the Unions NSW line.

Arithmetic on the National Executive was kindergarten stuff: the NSW Right + the Right obligated to the NSW Right (which would have been the entire national Right in a crunch) + what purports to be a Left + staffers and delegates concerned about precedent and proper process. Add all that up and you get a clear message to Kevin Rudd: stay well clear, my son. Given what Australians have since learned of a Prime Minister who shied away from 'the moral and economic challenge of our times', it was not likely that Rudd would expend political capital by placing his own authority on the line backing a cause that was already lost and a man who was beyond saving.

Iemma believed he had a solemn promise from the Prime Minister that Rudd would demand action from the National Executive to intervene on behalf of Iemma and cancel the decision of the NSW Annual Conference – silence in 2007 was in exchange for national intervention in 2008. Without national intervention, Iemma was entirely at the mercy of a majority at a properly constituted NSW Annual Conference. That majority was determined to deny a demand from the Prime Minister. To vote against a demand from a Prime Minister meant humiliating that Prime Minister and the Premier of New South Wales into the bargain. A majority of the Executive professed they would not resile, the Prime Minister would intervene at his peril. Rudd chose not to test the reach of his authority. Rudd has denied he ever made a binding commitment.

On the National Executive, the NSW Right could and did give notice of calling in favours owed by Right factions in the other five states. Iemma had no one to call, no favours to cash. The Right elsewhere, the ruling factions everywhere, they all knew that a Iemma triumph created a precedent most terrible for the party across Australia. The most obvious government that needed no encouraging that it was high and mighty was the government headed by Kevin Rudd. Each state machine is dedicated to electing a Labor government. None of the machines envisage that the government in their polity will declare independence from the party that made possible the election of each and every MP. The ruling machines tolerate the operational independence of Labor governments as long as it is leavened by homage to the party at election time and in conference speeches – these machine leaders, after all, universally aspire to be a part of just such an operation. It was otherwise to express independence so contemptuously. Iemma enjoyed moral support from the other premiers. None of those men and woman could deliver a vote.

The first days after the Annual Conference was a time of despond for the opponents of sale. The great victory looked like it counted for nothing. The press was united in its portrayal of the opponents of sale as self-serving and self-interested. The media misrepresented the opposition as being exclusively union-based. The press gallery ran a line that Iemma was showing real leadership by standing up to his own party while slagging Barry O'Farrell for taking seriously his constitutional responsibility to oppose the government. With many Liberal leaders, the temptation to take the easy cheers would not have been resisted. Barry O'Farrell eschewed the easy hurrahs in favour of the long game. His primary task was to bring down the government.

The Opposition's coming play was obvious. Yet the Iemma government and the media were expecting the Opposition leadership to make a decision that would (1) split the National Party from the Liberal Party; (2) divide the Liberal Party; (3) provide the government with a leave pass against the split in Labor ranks; (4) demonstrate that O'Farrell was a puppet of the traditional backers of his party; while (5) permitting Iemma to be the hero who stood up to pressures from his own party. Was there anyone in politics so stupid? Certainly not Barry O'Farrell. The media chose to interpret O'Farrell's elliptical statements as providing a green light after certain conditions were met.

Preparing for a departure

Bitar still believed he could talk Iemma into a peaceful departure. Talks continued through May and June to that end. Rees had to endure due diligence on his private life and finances, a far tougher scrutiny than any published profile. The exercise prepared the coming man for relating the narrative which he would duly have to present to the voters. Rees passed muster. His handlers did not want him to change. He had to be himself, swagger and all. Light grey suits and fawn gave way to dark. He started to wear better shirts, better ties.

Iemma was not going anywhere. Bitar was worldly aware: the brawl on electricity, while ever unresolved, secured Iemma's hold on the job. An outside prospect was trading off electricity for a change of leadership, which was not ever possible for reason that Robertson and Riordan, having come so far, were disinclined to make a compromise. Bitar wanted a fix to preserve Iemma's honour. Foley wanted Iemma gone. Bitar was coming to realise there would not be a gracious exit for his former friend. Bitar and Foley were seeking the same outcome though for different reasons. Bitar wanted primarily to avoid annihilation at the polls. Foley wanted the supremacy of Annual Conference recognised. Robertson was wanting the electricity bills defeated. Because so few had inside knowledge of the plot, unauthorised breakouts were a hazard. Hotheads in the unions wanted more drastic action. One wild moment was encouraging Paul Gibson to resign, bring on a by-election in which Robertson would stand, win and challenge Iemma. No one of significance supported that adventure.

Iemma flirted with the fates when he declined to attend the Administrative Committee. Bitar took off the gloves. The Caucus would resolve to act after a majority confronted hard truths and came to accept that Iemma had to go. Getting to that majority involved a campaign of one on one. Newspoll in state politics does not avail itself as strikingly as it does in federal. Newspoll for federal voting intentions and approval ratings appears every fortnight; for New South Wales voting intentions it is every two months. After publication, the state poll gets talked about for maybe two days. Being published in the *Australian*, many Labor MPs miss it. The Newspoll of 25 June 2008 was especially potent because it was published the day after Geoff Corrigan MP (Camden, highly marginal) told Iemma at a Caucus meeting that he (Iemma) was living in a parallel universe. Corrigan felt compelled to respond to his Premier's address that insisted everything was great. Newspoll showed Iemma sitting on 63 per cent disapproval. Angela D'Amore MP (Drummoyne, imposed) gave the leadership a big spray in the *Sun-Herald* not long after. Iemma did not doubt that these breakouts were orchestrated by the machine.

Bitar seized that moment to start seeing individual MPs. He spoke only about Newspoll, he did not use the private research, he did not advocate a move against Iemma. What Bitar did, most emphatically, was note that the MP he was talking to would be out at the next election. Bitar thought he was choosing his MPs with care. He misread two of them. Tanya Gadiel (Parramatta, imposed by the machine) reported the meeting to Iemma. Paul McLeay (Heathcote) blabbed to the St George *Leader*. In late July the metropolitan media ran big on Bitar's use of polling to undermine Iemma. The General Secretary did not brief the media at any time – standard operational procedure for undermining a leader. Nor did Bitar ever confirm that the numbers were bad for Iemma. (Neither of the informants scored a place in the Rees Cabinet.)

Iemma noted this increased activity of the General Secretary among MPs. Rumours were circulating of a petition to challenge the leader. Some MPs were mouthing off against Costa, a safer course than attacking the Premier. Iemma noted leaks to the media. The tabloids put fear into marginal seat holders with full-page spreads that carried their photos and polling which portended their destruction. The newspapers were speculating about the accession of Rees or Tebbutt.

The endgame begins

As the plot proceeded, life proceeded. The principals were not going to stop their daily business. Foley flew to Ireland for the 60th birthday of his father-in-law, his first holiday in a year. He turned off his mobile. The only number to reach him was for the phone on the farm where he was staying. During his absence, Costa had a monumental outburst: he tipped a bucket on Bitar and ALP Head Office. Reba Meagher and Kristina Keneally joined in the attack. All of Bitar's concern for secrecy had come to nought. These attacks betrayed a belief that the NSW Labor leadership is a presidential position.

Only one alternative name was in the public domain. Nathan Rees. No one decried Rees. The revelation caused moments of discomfort to him. He had to deny he was plotting. More than once he publicly pledged his loyalty to Iemma. He was repeating his assurances in private. Both Iemma and Rees knew the assurance applied only while Iemma held the position unchallenged. A two-prong coup would alter the equation. First prong was a vote to declare the position of leader vacant, second prong was a ballot to fill the vacancy. Rees would be a candidate in such a ballot. Iemma knew the score.

Hunger matters. Rees wanted the leadership. Federal Labor came to appreciate the importance of hunger after the years of Beazley's Shakespearian self-deprecation. Rudd positively lusted to be prime minister. It made a difference. Many MPs on the Right had an emotional attachment to Iemma. They hoped the ousting of Costa might do the trick. Rees did not talk about his intentions. He did not have to, given the machine was doing a lot of talking and more. The delicacies of personality and ambition could have blown him up at any time. With Rees breathing hard, his presence everywhere though out of sight, Iemma took no action that might have cruelled the succession of his only possible successor. The forbearance of Morris Iemma during those final weeks and days deserves enormous credit.

The self-proclaimed power-brokers, Eddie Obeid and Joe Tripodi, accepted the new leader had to be Rees. These two had become the axis of power within the Right caucus, creating enemies by their behaviour as surely as they did devotees. Their power is based on personal relations. Tripodi spends inordinate time delivering little things. He is there to assist in campaigns. Most importantly, like a village elder in Calabria, Tripodi is there to sort out differences. Obeid became father confessor to his fellow parliamentarians. People go in and out of Obeid's office all day long. He will be receiving one or more in his office while taking calls and serving food and drinks. People unload problems on him, the solver of problems personal and political. The sheer volume of the dealings of these two with members of the Right accorded them major influence over a majority of the Right caucus. A majority of the Right usually meant control of the parliamentary party.

There was no timetable beyond a sense that the paralysis could not continue past Christmas. It helped that the media wrote off the plotters. The number of MPs prepared to vote against the electricity bills had grown to a solid 14 from the 'Left' and five from the Right. The Opposition's opposition ensured defeat.

Defeating the electricity bills would certainly bring Iemma down. If the government somehow prevailed – if (for example) it abandoned honour and sought sale by way of an administrative order – the revulsion from the ALP would not be containable. The proponents of ignoring Conference did not reflect on what 'victory' would mean to the ALP. The Premier's private office was starting to fill with ex-operatives of Channel Nine, experts in shaping news for anodyne bulletins. Iemma was being hammered with the old chestnut that there was nothing wrong with the government, if only it could sell its message better. Bitar was highly critical of Iemma's communications people, as he was of much else in the office. Iemma invited in a Nine reporter he regarded highly and a gallery reporter. These arrivals were seen by some in the Labor Party as a sign that the government was preparing for a campaign without the Labor Party.

True or not, public funding and corporate donations have brought parliamentary parties to the point that, provided they secure those revenue sources, they do not need a connection of any kind to an extra-parliamentary organisation. The salaried political staff of elected governments will feel bound to ministers, not to the party of which they are members (if they are members). Ministerial staffers outnumber the staff of the ALP Head Office and all affiliated unions. Earning fabulous salaries, they are full-time political professionals, life's every breath is partisan politics. The effect of banning private donations is to liberate parties from the obligations attendant to fundraising. Tax dollars, it is argued, free parties of the need to sup with developers, hotel interests, vested interests. It also frees parties from dependence on their own members' energies. Parties not presently represented in a parliament will have a nightmare debut given that traditional fundraising will be denied them. Tax dollars flow retrospectively, according to the vote in the last poll. A new political movement, contesting seats for the first time, cannot receive donations, cannot raise funds. Behind the vaunting of the public funding reforms is an agenda to kill off competition to the major parties.

The Commonwealth or a state branch of the Labor Party may one day be the scene for combat over which entity – the parliamentary party or the extra-parliamentary organisation – is entitled to register the name of 'Labor' and 'Australian Labor Party'. It could happen in another party first.

Defeat in the Legislative Council

The leadership of the government preferred to reduce Caucus dissent to such tiny numbers that the Opposition would not matter. Pro-Iemma emissaries were offering ministries to all and sundry. Mick Veitch MLC told the media that he was charmed with assurances he had 'ministerial ability'. Veitch mocked the approach because he was aware around 50 other MPs had received similar entreaties. Where were all these vacancies going to come from? It was claimed that Costa had been threatening to cut off funding from those who voted against sale, a charge he denied. One does not doubt that Costa employed colourful language as he explained to MPs that the funding sought for a favoured project in one's electorate required the funds being available.

Nathan Rees kept his head down. He built relationships, he was seen to be hardworking, his office responded to enquiries from members of Caucus. Rees was available for fundraisers. He avoided the parliamentary bar and glad-handing. His chief of staff discussed at day's end the names of MPs who had contacted the office, what they were enquiring about, what the office was doing.

After Foley had returned from holiday in Ireland, Bitar went to the United States with his family. He was attending the Democrat Convention as an official observer. Foley came into his own. Such was the respect he had earned that the machine agreed that a notional Left-winger would have to be the Acting General Secretary. None of Foley's predecessors as the Left's man in Head Office had achieved this position, not John Faulkner, not Anthony Albanese, not Bruce Childs. The media, uninterested in detail, did not pause to reflect what Foley's accession meant about the state of the Right. Extra-parliamentary Labor (political and industrial) had achieved a unity unprecedented. United for one cause: bringing down a premier.

The introduction of the electricity bills in the Legislative Council was designed to ensure that the decision would be made in the chamber where the government conceded defeat was possible. Its strategy was reconvening the Parliament for a special sitting on 28 August. A combination of Nationals, Greens and Labor's Conference loyalists in certain opposition meant that the Liberals were going to determine the outcome. Costa did not waver from his belief that the Liberal Party's stated position was all bluster, for reason that its leadership must ultimately bow to ideological realities and to pressure from the big end of town. The night before the Opposition

Leader repeated that the Coalition parties were voting against. The announcement did not convince Costa, who insisted on a test of Liberal resolve on the floor of the Legislative Council. Iemma permitted Costa this last throw of the dice, though Iemma himself doubted that O'Farrell was going to do other than what his statements expressly said. Iemma and Costa, acting as a strategy group of two, had decided that, once the Opposition expressed hostile intent in their reply, the Government would withdraw the bills.

In his second reading, Costa gave his all once last time, speaking with the conviction of one who believes his words might yet change minds. In the second sentence of its reply, the Opposition affirmed it would be voting against. Costa accepted the bills were sunk and was not long in remaining in his seat. Departing the chamber while the reply continued is poor form in an institution which prides itself on observing courtesies. The Leader of Government Business, Tony Kelly, prepared to move an adjournment to formalise defeat. The Opposition wanted to extend their fun. On the procedural question, Labor's ranks stuck together to provide passage 19–18. The debate was all over in little more than an hour. Bernie Riordan was in the public gallery.

Costa panics the horses

On the following Friday evening, Costa rang Simon Benson of the *Daily Telegraph* and Imre Saluszinsky of the *Australian* to state on the record that all the ministers were going to have to take their medicine in a mini-budget. Spending was out of control, New South Wales was heading into a huge deficit. This was scarcely a situation newly arising or warranting such dramatic treatment. Costa threatened to resign if Cabinet did not embrace privatisation of the ferries ahead of the mini-budget – a threat that was contrary to the assurance he had provided the Board of Sydney Ferries at its inception in 2004. He was talking of big cuts in the public service. It was not possible to perceive how any of this would rebuild Labor's support in an electorate crying out for improved services. His distraught behaviour had everyone worried about what he might yet do or say.

Fairfax journalists had coincidentally gone out on strike, a B-team was writing any propaganda the government wanted. Costa's outburst enabled Bitar (from the United States) to renew dialogue with Obeid and Tripodi. That weekend Robertson spent in the Southern Highlands, minding his own business. Obeid and Tripodi came on board. In the nature of politics, Tripodi's self-image demanded that he be seen to be in charge. These two renowned players within the Right were joining the winning side. Their abandonment of Iemma did not cost Iemma his Caucus majority or hegemony within the Right. Their disposition, useful certainly, was not critical to the engineering of the coup. Their last-minute switch preserved the myth that they ran the show. Backing winners is astute practice in politics. They warrant full marks for the perception that they caused the switch, bonus marks for taking in the media.

> The State Government will force nervous upper house MPs into voting first on the $10 billion power sale in an 11th-hour bid to spare Morris Iemma a bloody brawl in the Legislative Assembly tomorrow morning. The tactic will force the first vote on the sale on to Mr O'Farrell's Liberal and National Party colleagues in the Legislative Assembly and force upper house Labor MPs to rethink plans of crossing the floor by not seeing colleagues vote in the lower house.
>
> (Simon Benson, *Daily Telegraph*, 27 Aug 2008)

Defeat of the electricity legislation walloped a critical mass of MPs with the undeniable truth that the government had lost its authority. Costa's rage had served to build a unanimity that he had to go. We need now to talk in days. The legislation was voted down on Thursday, 28 August. That afternoon the Cabinet adopted a Plan B which involved only the sale of retail – a proposal all but identical to that which the unions had put forward in 2007. A good number of Labor members were in the parliamentary bar for long and extensive celebration of the avoidance of a crisis that would not now test their loyalties. The joy was brought to an end by the convening of a special caucus at 5:00 pm to consider a new approach. Many of the Caucus had departed the building. The Cabinet needed to take some action, given the ratings agencies were demanding answers on how the government proposed to re-order its capital spending. Foley, Acting General Secretary with Bitar still overseas, seized the initiative by getting to Parliament House quick smart. He met with a majority of the 'Left' MPs who had been prepared to vote no. He persuaded them to accept the Cabinet's compromise. It was smart to be in a position to declare victory. Exploiting his position to the full, Foley insisted on seeing a reluctant Iemma. The war over electricity should end, Foley argued. Iemma agreed to discussions between Foley and Tripodi to talk through the process.

Foley believed Iemma would not step down until the electricity war ended. During the course of that night, Foley put this view to Bitar. On Friday morning, Foley gained the agreement of Robertson and Riordan. The device to preserve everyone's position was a spe-cial committee involving members of the ALP policy committees affected. This committee would test the Cabinet's Plan B against what ALP policy required. Foley went on ABC TV's *Stateline* on Friday 29 August to declare the war was over. He emphasised the party had won, the legislation was abandoned. With each of Bitar, Foley, Robertson, Riordan and Tripodi on-side, and Iemma acqui-escent, the temperature might have dropped considerably. Instead, Costa expostulated with Benson and Saluszinsky. A whole new war was starting. John Watkins was ringing other ministers to enlist their support to persuade Iemma to sack Costa.

From the United States, Bitar was talking turkey to Obeid and Tripodi during the weekend of 30–31 August. In Cabinet on Mon-day 1 September, John Watkins and others assailed Costa for his continuing impetuousity. Costa returned serve, then walked out. On Wednesday 3 September, Paul Keating rang Iemma to report a solid rumour that Tripodi and Obeid had switched support.

Keating had become a confidant of Iemma, his friendship was much valued. Iemma called in Tripodi to put the accusation to him. Tripodi denied it. Later that same Wednesday John Watkins, facing the prospect that Channel Ten was going to reveal his future employment by Alzheimer's Australia, convened a press conference to announce his resignation from Cabinet and Parliament. He had had enough. Iemma attended the press conference, the mutual affection was obvious. Watkins' resignation created a ministerial vacancy, its filling the trigger for a decision on the Iemma leadership. An unavoidable reshaping of the Cabinet was going to provide a mechanism to test the standing in Caucus of the Premier and those who were seeking to replace him. The test suited everyone. Iemma knew he had to make a play for affirmation of his authority.

A challenge was being prepared for Friday, 5 September, its exact mechanics uncertain. Barrie Unsworth had discovered the 'scarecrow' provisions in the ALP Rules about requiring Conference approval for a change of parliamentary leader. Unsworth alone believed that the words counted for anything. If a majority of Caucus votes against a leader, he or she is broken as and from that moment. Appealing to the machine for restoration underlines impotence. Iemma did not ever consider he could survive a hostile Caucus majority; he had based his defiance of Conference on preserving Caucus solidarity. On Thursday 4 September, the media wrote off the challenge.

Replacing Watkins might have brought out the ancient enmities within the 'Left'. Some have deluded themselves that the title of Deputy Premier confers leadership of the 'Left'. The Left in New South Wales has not had a leader since Jack Ferguson announced his retirement in 1983. Nathan Rees had the sense to declare no interest in the Deputy's spot. Carmel Tebbutt would take the position unopposed. Messiness on the sides did not inhibit majorities in the two sub-groups of the 'Left' to agree it was sensible to advance Tebbutt without opposition and retain Rees for the main prize. Ian Macdonald, an architect of the split within the Left in the 1980s, tried one last ploy to preserve disunity. He wanted a vote within the faction to decide who filled the vacancies, even though he had hitherto supported sub-group selection of candidates for sub-group vacancies.

In the state parliamentary Caucus the 'Left' faction does not matter; the only bodies that matter are the two sub-groups within the 'Left'. For two decades a collective voice coming from the 'Left' had been whatever survived the need for a consensus between people who otherwise despise each other. Macdonald had persuaded Robert Coombs (Wyong) to run for Watkins' vacancy. The persuasion did not matter when people of goodwill from both sub-groups agreed that the process that had preserved a semblance of unity should not now be abandoned on the eve of an unimagined triumph – Watkins' group would decide Watkins' replacement. After the 'Left' members had their faction meeting, they all went for a drink together. Unprecedented in decades.

Iemma's reshuffle rejected

On Thursday night the Right was in catharsis as the shape of Iemma's reshuffle became known. Iemma believed the re-allocation of portfolios was necessary to refloat the government. He was aware of the expectation that he would resign if electricity was not resolved. He considered electricity to have been settled. It was time to move on.

Iemma's closest friends in Cabinet, people genuinely hoping he might yet survive, became acquainted with his thoughts on the reshuffle. They endorsed the removal of Costa, a view on which the entire party had achieved unanimity. The dropping of Reba Meagher also enjoyed total support. At the end Meagher did not have a single advocate in her cause. These friends trembled when the Premier added his intention to drop Kevin Greene, a close personal friend, plus Graham West and Tony Kelly. Iemma reckoned that Greene had failed in Youth and Community Services. That Iemma was prepared to move against a man who was a friend reflected how serious he was about effecting change. West's sin was disagreeing with the Premier on issues and Iemma's belief West could not drive an agenda.

Friends pleaded with Iemma to forget the small targets and go after the big game – Joe Tripodi. If Iemma was seeking to show he was embarking on a completely new direction, he had to rid himself of Tripodi. Unaware that Tripodi and Obeid had reached an arrangement with the machine and those who would be advising the new premier, Iemma baulked. Tripodi had taken himself out of sight after the scandal in Wollongong broke. He had been cleared by the police and ICAC, pulled his head in, focussed on two small portfolios and was no more trouble. Tripodi might have been on the media's list for removal; he was not on the list of either the outgoing Premier or the new. Only that night did Robertson get word that the moment had arrived. Iemma would be executed at the Right's meeting next morning, come what may. For the first time since the factions conquered Caucus in 1984, people were resisting orders from above. Kelly and West were not going meekly to their fate. They were going to insist on a vote within the Right. Bitar was encouraging the resistance. So were Obeid and Tripodi. The fate of Morris Iemma came down to a stand taken by two junior ministers who were not going to be pushed around. There is a lesson here for all those who have stood aside in preselections because they accepted they could be pushed around by a faction leadership. Dare to win.

Around these unlikely heroes, a majority of the Right kicked back. A leader coming off a massive electoral victory is armed with moral suasion. A leader mid-term, polls languishing, does not possess that suasion. Not when you are acting in defiance of the Annual Conference, not when much of the party membership is alienated. In politics it is never easy to explain to a meeting why it is good to support the destruction of a fair proportion of those present. By making acceptance of his plan a condition for continuing as leader, Iemma created the mechanism for his own departure.

The leadership changes

The Right met in the Jubilee Room. In an echo of May's Annual Conference, the usual meeting place was unavailable. The room was a gift of the government to the legislature in 1906 to celebrate 50 years of responsible government. In this grand room, erected to fill in the space between the two chambers, the Right decided the fate of its leader, the party's leader, the state's Premier. He had come to work that day, and for some time previously, without feeling any pleasure in how he would fill in the hours ahead. A leader cannot long persist when he does not enjoy his job. The frustration had taken a heavy toll. On that Friday morning Iemma spoke to the Right without conviction, a speech in the monotone that frustration and stress had made the Premier's standard. The effect was to remind people that Iemma was not reaching the electorate. Iemma wanted support, his critics wanted him gone, the majority wanted the agony to end. Without the support of his factional colleagues, Iemma did not want to remain. Everyone understood the consequences of rejecting the reshuffle he was recommending.

The night before, Nathan Rees knew the leadership would crystallise in the next 24 hours. His phone was alive with incoming calls. At 3:45 am, John Della Bosca rang in a bid to become Treasurer, a request which revealed an acceptance that the leadership was going to change. In distant California, Karl Bitar was wide awake. While the Premier and his opponents were catching what sleep they could, Bitar discovered the battery in his mobile had run down. Not wanting to deprive his children of the joys of Disneyland, he took his battery with him with a view to recharging from whatever power point was available. When he discovered a power point in a merchandise store on the left of Main Street, Bitar plugged in. Being of Middle Eastern appearance, this behaviour did not go unnoticed. The staff of Disney took an interest, the level of interest escalated. What was this man up to? With the nation's security under threat, Bitar was instructed to remove his lead and leave the store. He was able to remain in Disneyland. As well he did not try to explain: being engaged in activities intended to bring down an elected government would have placed him in handcuffs. The party's leadership changed hands while Bitar was flying home.

If Iemma had entertained any doubts about the peril of his situation, a discussion that morning with Joe Tripodi and Eddie Obeid ended that doubt. Obeid and Tripodi revealed that they had switched, they could not deliver the numbers for the reshuffle proposed, the situation was a mess. Iemma was committed to proceeding. After an intense discussion in the Right caucus, it became clear that his proposals would fail. There was no show of hands. Iemma announced his resignation. He departed the room, followed out by David Campbell (Keira), Barbara Perry (Auburn) and John Hatzistergos MLC. Many were in tears. As the Premier was leaving he heard Tripodi say words to the effect of 'close the doors, it has to be Nathan'.

So it was. Word went around the meeting that Rees was the one, anointed by the machine and both factions. No one else was in the frame. While the Right caucus proceeded, Rees's feelings were of the surreal. He was waiting in his ministerial office on the ninth level of Parliament House, accompanied only by his chief of staff and Foley. They were standing in a large space looking a great deal larger because it had been stripped of all furniture, artwork and carpet ahead of refurbishing in the period between sessions when nothing much happens in the building. It was a matter of standing and waiting, reading a flood of text messages coming from downstairs, members of the Right making a play to the next leader. Deliberately, Rees has not preserved those messages. The traffic was one-way. Rees could not acknowledge. The messages provided a narrative of the drama unfolding two floors below. After a good while a second flood of messages reported that the Premier had announced his resignation, followed by another flood that the Right was electing someone from outside its ranks as party leader and Premier. Rees considered for just a moment the enormity of what had befallen him, before making just the one phone call out. It was very short. 'Stace, I'm going to be Premier.'

Iemma's staff found out what was happening by turning on radios and looking at the net. The ALP Caucus met soon after the Right had done its business. The meeting started late for reason of the doing of that other business. Rees and the members of his faction waited patiently for the Right to join them. The Right arrived about 15 minutes late. John Watkins, outgoing Deputy, and Morris Iemma, outgoing Premier, arrived together and left together. The atmosphere was subdued. There were more tears. It was a matter-of-fact occasion. The 'Left' filled the two vacancies that were its to fill. The Premier tendered his resignation. Iemma remained while Nathan Rees was elected.

In accordance with Caucus Rules, the returning officer read out all of the names of the members of Caucus in alphabetical order. A candidate nominates by answering to the call of his or her name. Rees alone responded. He was elected unopposed. The applause was polite. No one was in the mood for exuberance. It began to dawn on members of the Right what they had done. They had rejected one of their own in order to install a Left-winger, as the Right considered Rees to be.

In his acceptance speech Rees stated the need to put an end to the open warfare. He asserted Labor could win the next election – by discussion, fighting on the ground, a superior policy program. The hostile media environment was unlikely to let up. The party would go over and under the mainstream media by way of community cabinets and direct engagement with opinion leaders. Cautious about his prospects, the premier-elect warned in express terms that an immediate bounce in the polls was unlikely. The government had to grind out its recovery week by week. He did not speak from notes. After the speech were formalities and photos. His first act was to visit Iemma in the Premier's office in Parliament House. Iemma received other visits of consolation and best wishes. He then departed Parliament House to hold a press conference at the Governor Macquarie Tower, after which he signed a letter of resignation for delivery to Government House.

Bitar and Foley did not want any sort of interval between the downfall and the accession, just in case mischief-makers within the Right sought to regroup. Getting the Right to swallow a notional Left-winger was a big enough step without allowing a night's sleep for reconsideration. The journey to Government House for the swearing-in proceeded with the same urgency.

The Lieutenant-Governor, Jim Spigelman CJ, had been advised some time earlier that he would be required at Government House during Friday morning. The Premier's Department was expecting that the Lieutenant-Governor would be presiding over the reconstruction of the Iemma government. His task was somewhat different. Morris Iemma formally resigned, then advised the Lieutenant-Governor to call on Nathan Rees. Rees arrived shortly after with his deputy, Carmel Tebbutt, plus spouses. Those two and they alone were sworn in. Between them they held all portfolios in the New South Wales government. For that day and the weekend following, the state was governed by a two-person Cabinet.

The story is contained in the *NSW Government Gazette*. Jim Spigelman had been there before, in the study at Yarralumla in Canberra in December 1972 when Sir Paul Hasluck granted a commission to the duumvirate of Gough Whitlam and Lance Barnard. Spigelman was a senior member of Whitlam's staff during Opposition. He was invited to witness that moment in history. The immediate swearing-in of September 2008 underlined the importance of speed, how critical it was that the choice of the Caucus was vested with formal, irreversible authority. The Premier's Department docked pay for those three days; the gap will have a minute effect on superannuation payouts. Records of the government will need to show that all its ministers, bar Rees, broke their period of service.

Morris Iemma returned to his home at Narwee in pouring rain. His children greeted him with high-fives, each aware their father was no longer Premier.

Chapter 6

The protracted fall of Nathan Rees

Karl Bitar was home from California in time for the Saturday of negotiations ahead of Caucus on Sunday. Lots of precedents were being set. An agreed list of names had to go to the Right caucus. The 'Left' had already decided on its nominations. The new Premier and the General Secretary met at the Concord West home of Luke Foley, an emphatic tribute to Foley's effectiveness during the previous weeks. The meeting settled most of what went forward to the Right. Rees explained the role of Bitar:

> You can imagine the machinations and the exchanges that have gone on. I have kept well and truly out of it from the outset. My instructions to NSW General Secretary Karl Bitar were: 'You manage this process. You keep bringing me back the list and I'll keep sending it back to you until I've got a list I'm comfortable with.'

The Premier devolved to the General Secretary the role of co-ordinator general for the Right. Given the Right was incapable of providing a leadership contender and had fallen to pieces, Bitar was assuming the role that used to be played by Carr and Iemma, augmented down the years by the likes of John Aquilina, Michael Egan, Richard Amery, Paul Whelan, John Della Bosca as well as Obeid and Tripodi. The Premier was now in a position similar to Neville Wran: he was not a member of the Right, he did not belong to a faction. Unlike Wran, Rees did not have an election victory behind him. He was wholly reliant on Bitar delivering the goods. Rees' involvement, while standing apart, was as far as he could go in seeking a congenial ministry. He could not rely on the parliamentary Right in its traumatised state to do anything sensible.

In the circumstances Bitar did a fine job. For those who still expected Tripodi to hit the wall, a connection with political reality is required. Consider the advantages cooperation conferred on both Tripodi and the backers of Rees. Tripodi knew Rees was going to win with or without him. Why not cooperate, cut a deal on the side, promise ongoing loyalty to the new regime? For Rees and co, why not accept the offer of cooperation, bring Tripodi onto the cart? No one knew how badly the day might play if the dumped gave vent to their feelings. The loyalty of Iemma was a given. Costa could do anything, so could Meagher. No one cared about them or what they might say or do. Tripodi was another matter: alienate Joe and you could create a cavern on the backbench to focus disaffection. The fear was an ongoing campaign of whispers to the media that thrived on that sort of stuff. Best to kill off the possibility. Rees doubted he would lead Labor to a general election with Tripodi on board, a matter for time and events to resolve. Rees was hoping that an improvement in Labor's electoral prospects would translate into an expanded personal authority.

The Bitar ticket, approved by Rees, preserved the omissions of Costa and Meagher. Advised the night before by Iemma that he was dropping him from his ticket, Costa had made a parting gift to the future of the government by convening a media conference to share information about the state's finances. Costa was resigned to his fate. Reba Meagher was otherwise.

It began with a stroll

The new government began with a stroll. To Government House for the swearing-in, a scene of vibrant renewal as Ministers and spouses with children in tow made this solemn moment a family occasion. A fine image was captured by cameras still and moving of a government that was starting over again. The new Premier and his team had no illusions about the depth of the hole they were in. Thirteen years in government wears out the tolerance for shortcomings and delay. Earlier patience had gained no reward. The circumstances of the victory in 2007 were setting up Labor for an all-time hiding. The electorate had been forgiving, more than generous in years past. Forgiveness was done. There was no more to be given.

The objective peril of his situation, electoral and internal, was a factor in Rees' approach from day one. In his Caucus and Cabinet there were no mentors, no one who had done it before, no one who had known the loneliness of leadership and what it could demand of a person. Only two in the Rees Cabinet had known Opposition, both from the backbench in the Legislative Council. Although the government was 13 years old in 2008, a combination of retirements and wastage had left it with less experience of life and politics than at its outset. Within no time the Cabinet would be down another three. Rees lacked a protective shield inside the Caucus, except from Tripodi – for which the price was ultimately too high. Iemma and Rees both suffered from the absence of experienced hands, those who had been there before and had no realistic expectation of return, comfortable in their identities, honoured to be of service.

The transformation of politics from a lifetime career of public service to but one phase of a career trajectory, ever upward, has meant that the parliamentary parties have lost much of their memory bank. By contrast, Neville Wran, on being elected in 1976, had been able to draw on the experiences of Jack Renshaw, a former Premier who had been an MP since 1941, and Pat Hills, a former leader who had been in Parliament since 1954. Most of all

Wran could rely on his deputy, Jack Ferguson, in the Parliament since 1959, a redoubtable warrior of a thousand wars, who acted as Wran's eyes and ears, protector and conscience. No one could ever come at Neville except through Jack, so no one came at Neville. For his first three years as leader Bob Carr had Barrie Unsworth, plus his own invaluable seven years in Opposition, the blessings of which were not apparent at the time. In Andrew Refshauge, Carr had a deputy who had passed those seven years in Opposition alongside him and all their time together in Parliament. The deputies for Iemma and Rees took office on the same day as their leaders. Even with Tripodi totally loyal, Rees confronted a simmering cauldron from day one which could not wait to tear him down.

Nothing prepares a premier for what is ahead. Nathan Rees had been in Parliament for all of 18 months. He had to begin the government as if anew. Given the consummate attention to the detail of those who plotted his accession, the backers of Rees were unprepared for what was required to lead a government. Masterly inaction during the downfall of Iemma meant that Rees could scarcely have convened workshops of allies to prepare a plan for government action.

The elevation of Rees had depended on the assertion of the paramount power of the ALP machine, carried into a deadly final play by a rare unity between the extra-parliamentary factions. John Della Bosca was unable to contain his resentment at being passed over without a moment's consideration. Rees had guaranteed Frank Sartor's hostility by dropping him from Cabinet. Within days, Rees had demanded the resignation of another minister from the Right for his private behaviour, followed by another Right-wing minister for an alleged offence in public. Ongoing protection from outside Parliament was needed to put down grumblings by elements of the Right faction.

Rees had been elected leader on the principle of the only man standing. Unless he achieved fabulous numbers in the published polling, that external protection needed to be massive and terrifying to deter anyone contemplating a move against him. The parliamentary Right, broken and lacking a credible alternative, could not move until someone credible emerged from within its ranks in the Legislative Assembly. John Della Bosca convinced himself that he could become the leader of the party and head a government while remaining a Member of the Legislative Council. It was a delusion he alone entertained. The parliamentary Right would not move until and unless authorised by the machine leadership of the Right. The difficulties with the Iemma leadership had altered the basic discourses of the parliamentary party. Altered entirely was the degree of involvement by the party machine in Caucus business. Rees expected the resolute protection of Bitar, on the realistic expectation that the author of his accession would want to ensure the success of his deed.

Very much aware of his precarious status, never once confident he would survive to the next election, Rees set about building relationships wherever he could. Camps had developed over and above factions, the Right caucus was balkanising, the peril of the objective electoral situation affected all thinking. A bruised Right was also a fractured Right. Rees set about accommodating splinters and the disaffected. The shorthand description of the tendencies within the Right broke the faction into 'Trogs' and 'Terrigals', labels which defined their willingness to work with the Right's extra-parliamentary machine – not that anyone within the Right was all that courageous in resisting that machine, not after the fall of Iemma. The number of candidates imposed without local membership support plus MLCs had altered fundamentally the character of the parliamentary Right.

Rees found these labels of faction and sub-faction useless. What was more useful was to list MPs according to the response to the question not being asked: would you back any of Sartor, Della Bosca and, later, Keneally against Rees? Policy was not a factor. At no time in his premiership did Rees commit an act that could be described as Left, other than such acts as Carr or Iemma would have been comfortable with. It did not matter. Those working against Rees would seize on anything, real or fictitious, to undermine him.

The refrain was consistent – he is from the Left. The Premier was under pressure daily. Whereas Carr and Iemma employed staff with loyalties to the 'Left' without a murmur, such people were fingered by Rees' critics as evidence of what was wrong with the government.

Occasionally, Rees gave vent to his anger about this undermining. He was intending to rely on trust and the evidence of his good intentions. Rees took the view that trust is the only long-term way to combat disloyalty and treachery. Since the end of the Lang era, trust from the leader to his troops has resulted in a full reciprocation. Trust was not sufficient in the Caucus of 2007 to 2009. No matter how hard a leader tries, he or she will make mistakes. The key has been to identify those mistakes and fix them. In ordinary times, if a leader stumbled, those around him provided support and mopped up. With Iemma and Rees the situation was the reverse. Every stumble was magnified deliberately. Caucus morale, low to begin, did not rise. Rees was deeply frustrated by the white-anting. He claimed his morale was unaffected, for reason that it is impossible to be disappointed when you have zero expectations. If, at times, Rees seemed close to exploding, it is scarce surprising. His naturally exuberant personality was easily interpreted as a rage contained.

The media encouraged the undermining. The electricity crisis had encouraged everyone with an opinion to speak out. All too many enjoyed seeing their words, though not their names, out there. You did not require all that many MPs breaking ranks to create an appearance that the Caucus was beset with division, even if the division in the early days of the Rees leadership was no more than a coterie. Reporters could achieve their ends with the canard: 'I've heard this. What do you say?' A leader will soon enough be under siege if he has no means of putting down those working against him. The machine was neither able nor willing to take the action required against dissidents. Beside Rees in Cabinet sat John Della Bosca. The Premier could not help noting that his Health Minister left his diary open on the cabinet table: there was nothing in it but luncheon appointments. (The Minister's office doubtless kept his official appointments in a separate book.)

The props depart

The props of support for Rees outside Parliament proceeded to depart the field. The month following, on 17 October, Karl Bitar was elected as ALP National Secretary, although he had given assurances that he was in the New South Wales job for the duration – that is, until the 2011 state election. His departure was complete in every sense. Rees did not again hear from his champion in any material way once Bitar left New South Wales. His departure unexpected, no plans had been made for the succession for reason no one was thinking about succession for a good while yet.

The Right took soundings to determine the successor to Bitar. The selection process did not include the present officials in the ALP office, none of whom was general secretary material. Bitar had sounded out Matt Thistlethwaite, an assistant secretary of Unions NSW, the officer deputed by Robertson to wage the electricity campaign. Robertson supported this choice. At October's beginning, Robertson was expecting to be at Unions NSW for the long haul, having been thwarted in his bid to become Secretary of the ACTU by elements of his own faction. In the absence of other contenders, Thistlethwaite took over the key job in the ALP machine, the first General Secretary since 1969 not to have risen through the ranks of Head Office. Thistlethwaite had to master a job completely outside his experience. His first attendance at the ALP Administrative Committee was as General Secretary, a novice in the body where all previous occupants had enjoyed the advantage of having witnessed how their predecessor did the job. Thistlethwaite did not shake the perception of being uncomfortable.

Thistlethwaite has a conventional party background of the modern era – that is, a denizen of the political class who has enjoyed continuous employment inside the Labor movement. Thistlethwaite is a surf lifesaver, loves sport and gives every appearance of being a normal, well-adjusted Australian. His first job of consequence was on the staff of the Australian Workers' Union during which time he built the branches in Kingsford-Smith with a view to succeeding Laurie Brereton as the federal member. Brereton out-manoeuvred Thistlethwaite by delaying the announcement of his resignation so that, with the support of the federal leader, Mark Latham, the National Executive could impose Peter Garrett. The gambit was payback for Thistlethwaite's support for the candidate who purged Brereton's sister in the state seat of Heffron. That other candidate was one Kristina Keneally. Thistlethwaite responded by taking on the job of campaign director for Garrett. He departed the AWU to take a senior position with Unions NSW. That stint convinced the managers of the Right that he was the best available for the main job in the ALP office at a time when no one else was seriously in the frame.

The first person Thistlethwaite called upon was the Premier. The two men scarcely knew the other, so they had to establish a relationship from scratch. Rees knew that the ALP President, Bernie Riordan, was not supportive, a disposition which evolved into open hostility. Thistlethwaite, aware that his continuing employment depended on the support of the Right – that is, good notices coming from the big Right unions and the leadership of Unions NSW – did his best in serving a premier and party leader unsupported by a significant proportion of the faction on whose support his own future depended. Inexperienced in party office politics, Thistle-thwaite sought to avoid a conflict of loyalties by avoiding conflict. That task became increasingly difficult as more and more within the Right wanted to end the Rees leadership.

October 2008 was an active month. Rees invited John Robert-son to take Costa's vacant seat in the Legislative Council. There was surprise Robertson accepted the entreaty, given he was genuinely doubtful about the wisdom of this course. His acceptance was an error that played to the mournful tune of his enemies who had asserted from the outset that Robertson's opposition to privatisa-tion was based on personal ambition. On the backbench Robertson remained while attitudes tempered. His role in the fall of Iemma meant he could not enter the ministry early for fear of a payback play which would double as a test of Rees' authority. When Robertson did enter Cabinet, he had responsibility for prisons. The champion of anti-privatisation pushed through measures to privatise corrective services.

The Premier was the biggest loser from these departures and arrivals. Rees had induced his champion in the unions to abandon his union post at the same time he had lost his champion in the ALP office. Rees also erred in the management of senior personnel in the public service. The Director-General of the Premier's Department, whom he had inherited from Morris Iemma, chose to resign when Rees announced major cuts in the Senior Executive Service without consulting her. Rees did not accept the resignation and asked for a reflection. She paused for that reflection before insisting that she preferred to resign. Her departure began a procession of resignations from senior ranks.

The replacement was John Lee, a public servant well connected with Labor who had headed multiple agencies for short periods during Labor's years. Whatever he brought to the job it included none of the authority expected of the person who is the institutional head of the state's public service. Even in Rees' private office, there was wonder at the appointment. In the senior ranks of the public service, the feeling was profound disappointment. None of which mattered: Lee enjoyed the support of the one opinion that counted. Rees considered Lee to possess a good policy mind and analytical skills. Other ministers thought Lee forgot his place. They were unimpressed that he weighed into debates with a gusto inappropriate for one who was not a minister. Rees and Lee would go down together, the Premier effectively blind-sided about the mood of the public service. A premier needs a confidant at the head of his own department who can advise what the ranks are really feeling. It did not help that Rees had so recently been a ministerial staffer himself.

Loyalty persuaded Rees to remain with the chief of staff who had come with him. Rees wanted to stick with a man of unimpeachable loyalty, a good friend and fine person. He was deliberately favouring loyalty over experience. Expecting staff to take a bullet for him, he was most reluctant to move anyone out. Realities, nonetheless, dictated he needed another person to run his office. Where Iemma had looked beyond New South Wales to find Kaiser, Rees reached into the recent past of the Carr government. Graeme Wedderburn had served Carr exceptionally well, right up to the day of Carr's resignation. Wedderburn had then followed Carr out of the government. He had gained a lucrative position firstly in a bank, and then in one of the electricity companies, both on salaries several leagues ahead of what he had known. The machine intervened to get Wedderburn back. Arbib rang Wedderburn continuously. Encouraged by this activity, Rees began negotiations. It was important for Wedderburn to discover what Rees wanted from him. Wedderburn wanted to return. Carr entered the equation as broker. The three men met discreetly in Carr's office in Bligh Street, a short distance from the Governor Macquarie Tower.

The deal struck to lure the return of Wedderburn went beyond money. He was honoured to serve a new Labor government; he was delighted that his past service was recognised by the Premier (whose boss he had been when Rees worked for Carr). As the price for his return Wedderburn exacted the promise of a winnable spot on Labor's Senate ticket. The deal would only be binding if Rees and Wedderburn both worked out. Wedderburn returned on 5 February 2009, five months into the Rees leadership, a lot of time forfeit, a lot of momentum lost.

Wedderburn made a big difference. He came with a strong reputation after his service with Carr, an impeccable heritage and standing within the Right. For Rees, Wedderburn's appointment served the dual purpose of achieving maximum efficiency for his office and sending a message to his critics within the Right. He was a valuable personal link to Roozendaal. Wedderburn found many hundreds of good process decisions buried in the unending talk of leadership. He also found a premiership qualitatively different to the model forged by Bob Carr, who had been the pre-eminent person in his government. The ALP office thought it was running this government.

The most striking difference between the two governments was the authority Carr had asserted was gone. From afar, Wedderburn had noted how the activities of the party machine had drained power from Morris Iemma. He had signed up to help out a new Premier who was exhausted by the strain of the past months. Wedderburn endeavoured to win back control of the government to the government. For starters, he reintroduced the 6:00 am telephone hook-up with all the press secretaries and media advisers employed in ministerial offices. Thistlethwaite was welcome to listen in. After a short while, Thistlethwaite dropped out. Whereas Arbib had pioneered a trespass unprecedented on the time of a premier – one which Bitar had witnessed and adopted – Thistlethwaite brought no such experiences with him. Wedderburn detected a party officer who did not seek to be powerful.

Leaking by ministers against opponents had reached endemic levels. Leaks from within Cabinet were commonplace. Chance remarks, damaging out of context, were soon passed to friendly reporters. Circumspection had taken the place of robust, productive discussion. A malevolent force handed over the private contact details of ministers and senior staff. The disciplines which Carr had imposed and Wedderburn had earlier enforced were fond memories. Ministers kept a second mobile to make calls private and sensitive, fearful that their use of government-issue mobiles meant that an officer in the Premier's Department – where all bills went for payment – could trawl for an unfriendly purpose. Office computers inspired the same fear given they were all connected, the mainframe subject to central scrutiny. However misplaced, that such fears were abroad was evidence of corrosive dysfunction at the top.

Attending focus groups in his first weeks was the means by which Wedderburn sought to learn the depth of the electoral problems. Thistlethwaite convened groups in western Sydney and Gosford, two groups each night, one following the other, a gender balance of groups of eight or nine people, aged late 20s to 40s and employed. The data were powerful. The findings were every bit as striking as those that had persuaded Bitar to take down Iemma. The groups could name without prompting the leaders from the former government, adding a galaxy of new names. Unprompted naming is unusual in such groups. None of what these people said was flattering.

Focus groups will, at best, draw out the perceptions of those unconnected with politics. Chosen for their ordinariness, these voters will not understand the detail of public policy, the difficulties in making hard choices about resource allocation and the difficulties of delivering services. Perceptions will be driven by vicarious knowledge – that which group members have heard or seen in the media. Focus groups are based on the precept that you cannot go wrong if you give the punters what they want. The manifest decline in political courage, the absence of decisions for the long-term, is the result of a narcotic reliance on focus groups and qualitative polling. Contemporary political leaders dare not seek to persuade the electorate that it is wrong and why.

Whereas Bitar had wanted a wholesale purge, Wedderburn could not cause the machine to acknowledge that there was a problem of at least perception, the first step to addressing the unpalatable question of what those running the party might do. Carr in 2003 had struck down Obeid immediately after his election victory and otherwise acted to renew his government as it commenced its third term. Rees, minus a mandate of any kind, could not act without total machine backing. He did not have that backing. He did not act.

The honeymoon ends

The prospect of a recovery in the published polls was always unlikely. The mini-budget of 11 November 2008 killed the honeymoon stone dead. In his reshuffle, Rees had appointed Eric Roozendaal as Treasurer, a person who was certain to support the line coming out of Treasury. He compounded that difficulty by appointing Joe Tripodi as Assistant Treasurer. These two men in combination were an alternative source of authority to the Premier, the axis of authority within Cabinet. Through the whiphand of finance, Rees was circumscribed. The Budget Committee of Cabinet became masters of the domain, often the location of a battle for supremacy between Roozendaal and Tripodi. Roozendaal became so impressed with notices about himself that he imagined himself as another who might replace Rees. Della Bosca remained resentful about all three. In this sub-committee he had most cause to be reminded that each of Carr, Iemma and now Rees had deliberately overlooked him for Treasurer.

The mini-budget was essentially the response to the problem in the state's finances first highlighted by Michael Costa. Rees felt the need to proceed with rising expenditure. The measures in the mini-budget were counterintuitive to a government languishing in the polls. The electorate had come to believe that the government had not been spending sufficiently on basic services, and was not following through on announcements made about long-term projects. The mini-budget simultaneously axed the North West Metro, the South West Rail Link and other rail duplication. It introduced new fees for motorists, eliminated grants to parents of schoolchildren, placed a freeze on a substantial part of public service recruiting, while cutting the Senior Executive Service by 20 per cent. Land tax and property transfer fees went up. Nurses lost overtime, while fees went up for specialists using public facilities. A new range of public assets was going to be sold including NSW Lotteries, the electricity retailers and sites earmarked for future power stations.

A fatal problem for the government, inherited from its predecessors, flowing to its successor, was that people stopped believing grand announcements, especially on public transport. Another change of minister, a change of Treasurer, a change of Premier, chill winds, new enthusiasms – any and all could cause a project launched with fanfare to be killed by a press release. One tally of major rail projects announced over 15 years counted 12 that had been cancelled – including revivals being cancelled again. No project was certain to proceed. Private party polling revealed that announcements in and of themselves were a negative for the government, even if the announcements contained unequivocal good news. The electorate had stopped believing anything was going to happen.

The crisis of all state governments is the need to fund basic services. Trying to meet that need had driven Morris Iemma on his fateful course. The Rudd government elected in November 2007 had expressly declined to offer assistance to benighted state governments of Labor persuasion in improving those basic services. The Commonwealth could rely on revenues from income tax, company tax, capital gains tax, streams of revenues from the export of metals and minerals. The states were limited to regressive taxes based on property, transfers of assets, payrolls, various licence fees and a pernicious regime of taxes derived from gambling in all its forms, plus the GST. The states depended on the volume activity of the wider economy. The states could not meet their commitments without Commonwealth reimbursements of taxation mixed with heavily tied special-purpose grants. Talk of cooperative federalism coming from Rudd was hollow; heroic words conjured for a campaign. Giving oneself a prize for economic management sounded like vanity to a voter who lived in an Australian city relying on a state government to get them to and from work, quickly, safely and efficiently. It looked worse than vanity for those hoping for reliable hospital and health care. It was as if commuters at railway stations and bus stops and people needing health services were citizens of another country. (When, finally, the Rudd government announced its hospital package in 2010, it offered no additional money to the states. The premiers of the larger states forced real additional funding as the price of their eventual support.)

Eleven days after the mini-budget, the American financial services giant Lehman Brothers collapsed. Australia was suddenly in a different world. The Rudd government announced a massive stimulus package, a new scale of public spending without regard to keeping the Commonwealth budget in surplus. The strategy behind the New South Wales mini-budget looked horribly out of place. None of that federal spending assisted the states and territories in rebuilding basic services.

The mini-budget ended the prospect that Rees could put together the support needed to take Labor back in front. The government had remained determined not to suffer a downgrade by the ratings agencies. That is, the government did not want an external agency – a private corporation not answerable to the electorate – to alter the ratings which determined the interest rate upon which it could borrow money. The public sector and public services have suffered grievously from the aversion of modern governments to take on debt to fund social programs and infrastructure. The aversion has become tantamount to a diminishing of parliamentary sovereignty. In accepting this aversion, Rees was exposing the difficulties of someone nominally from the Left in challenging the assumptions of how governments might finance their works. In the world of ratings, the New South Wales government scored a win. Its rating improved from 'negative outlook' to 'stable'. Rees met the ratings agencies personally so they understood the government was serious about fiscal discipline.

Winning these brownie points counted not a jot in the electorate. Rees had begun behind in the polls; he remained behind. After Iemma's plunge in the Newspoll satisfaction rating to 26 per cent in the July–August 2008 research, Rees made an immediate leap to 39. He did not again reach that number; in May-June 2009 he touched 30. His dissatisfaction went from a low of 26 at the beginning to twice that number by the end of his premiership. The primary vote for Labor and the two-party preferred vote was the stuff of death. Support for the ALP had collapsed from the final poll findings under Iemma of 33 per cent to a miserable 29 per cent for Rees in September–October 2008. The numbers were scarcely surprising given the electorate had been treated to a public show of a party and government in meltdown. Rees took the primary voting intentions above 30 per cent for the first 10 months of 2009, after which the ALP dropped back to 26. The plotters took comfort from the absence of any upward movement in Rees' poll numbers. A government in a terminal phase suffers from people within its ranks who lack any sense of consequence. It would have been remarkable if any leader could have turned around the standing of a government bitterly divided against itself 13 years, going on 14, after it had come to power.

The narrative of the 15 months of the Rees leadership is one of internal division. In not one week in all that time did Nathan Rees enjoy clear air. Always he was dealing with a crisis of his own party's making or a difficulty in public policy that confirmed the public's sense that the government was not in charge. Add the preceding 16 months of unending destabilisation inflicted on Morris Iemma from mid-2007 and the picture is a horror. For some 31 continuous months the energies of several MPs and ministers were devoted to destroying their parliamentary leader. Given the strain, Iemma and Rees did well to contain their tempers in public and, for most of the time, in private.

The media loved the gore. All journalists had to do was sit and wait for bile to drip on to their keyboards. Elements of the media covered the difficulties in ALP leadership like troubles in a royal marriage. Any whisper was good enough to go with. Reporters exulted in stories of unlikely combinations at lunch without considering that the lunchers had come together for no reason beyond being reported. It registered not that none of the manoeuvrings by Labor MPs mattered, nothing mattered until the machine decided that Rees was no longer worth protecting. Purposeful energy went into persuading the General Secretary to abandon Rees and persuading the machine's leadership group that the General Secretary needed persuading. Activities of MPs mattered little until they were assured they would be backed by the machine in the adventure under contemplation.

A deal for springing at Annual Conference

Annual Conference loomed as large for Rees in 2009 as it had for Iemma the year before. That Rees was not in conflict with his party was entirely irrelevant. An annual conference so late in the year – the latest since the War – provided a punctuation point for plotters and the Rees group alike. If Rees should continue into 2010 – bring himself inside one year of a general election – the timing of a challenge would need to take account of the space, if any, for a new leader to build any sort of presence. Rees settled the matter by deciding to make Conference an occasion for rebirth. He opted for a remote outside chance of survival by taking action against his troubles instead of succumbing to the certain fate of inaction: being torn to pieces by wolves on a deserted snow drift. He had reached the point that there was no point. Going into the 2009 Annual Conference, Rees recognised three moments of extreme hazard ahead: (1) the weekend, (2) the parliamentary session, (3) a challenge in late February. He was assuming that the General Secretary was sticking by him. Rees had good reason for that confidence.

Two Saturdays prior to Annual Conference – 31 October – a meeting was held at the Premier's office which lasted from 1:00 to 3:00 pm. Present were Nathan Rees, Graeme Wedderburn, Matt Thistlethwaite, Luke Foley and Senator John Faulkner – the last a friend of Rees since childhood, present to confirm the gravity of the business under discussion. All were dressed casually. Mark Arbib was invited but was unable to attend. Under discussion was the intention of the Premier to use his address to Conference to demand changes to party Rules to confer on the Premier the right to select and sack his ministers. Rees made it expressly clear that he proposed to use that power forthwith so as to sack Tripodi and others. In expressing frankly how exposed that move would make him, Rees asked for an open pledge of support to come through the contumely ahead. Foley committed the party machine to back the move. At which all eyes turned to Thistlethwaite. Foley had spoken well outside his station, as well he knew. Of the people in the room only Thistlethwaite might command the big battalions in the Right-wing unions. Thistlethwaite nodded his consent to the commitment and said yes.

Secrecy was of the essence to achieve surprise at the Conference, though catching such operatives by surprise could well spook the big battalions to vote against. Union officials were not going to appreciate being kept in the dark, not they who controlled the party and Annual Conference. Arbib was brought into the secret on the Monday following. Thistlethwaite and Arbib decided they would tell the Right that they had only found out about these plans on the morning of Conference. They were counting on the drama of the moment – the enormity of rejecting a premier's plea – to force the Right's approval. For both men it was a huge call.

The proposition to afford the parliamentary leader the right to choose his front bench had been discussed over several weeks by Rees, Wedderburn, Thistlethwaite and Foley – a group which had been meeting weekly for some time, as near to being a Rees support group as Rees ever knew. The proposal had its beginnings in the successful bid by Kevin Rudd for such authority prior to the 2007 federal election and implemented immediately after his government's election. It had been under active consideration for all of 2009. Decisive action on ministerial selection was agreed at an earlier lunch in *Capitan Torres*, a Spanish restaurant in Liverpool Street close to the ALP office, attended by Thistlethwaite, Foley and Wedderburn. Thistlethwaite was central to the planning from day one.

Annual Conference, November 2009

Once again Annual Conference took place away from the Sydney Town Hall. This time in the Sydney Entertainment Centre. Stung by the criticisms of the inappropriateness of the auditorium at the Convention Centre, the organisers sought to replicate the seating layout at Town Hall. The large open arena was divided in two, one half faced the other half, eight rows of seats, with a lectern in the middle of the floor. The result was an impressive facsimile of the Town Hall of fond memory. On the stage were the party officers – President, General Secretaries, Assistant General Secretaries. Once, the ALP had two vice-presidents who were both major identities; now they seem to have 28 of them, all non-entities. A television camera was on the left. A large screen sometimes showed the floor speaker. The media sat on the two sides of the stage, they did not enjoy a line of sight to the stage speaker or the floor.

The Premier's address took place late on Saturday morning. At 9:00, before the Conference opened, the party officers of the Right plus John Robertson held a meeting on the stage. The gathering came inside the knowledge of the Rees' request and were required to make a response. Their call was vital. Without the support of the Right's officers, the troops would certainly vote the proposal down. Matters were so dire that not even the Right leadership could be sure their recommendation would carry the faction. John Robertson was one deeply disturbed by this bid for extended power. Phone calls of the day previous now became clear to him. A meeting a few days earlier with Rees, Wedderburn, Mark Lennon (Robertson's successor at Unions NSW) and Thistlethwaite had disappeared from the Robertson diary. He could see that the meeting had proceeded deliberately in his absence so as to lock in Lennon. The gambit succeeded. Robertson was not impressed that Lennon was committed. It is hard to say no to the Premier, Lennon explained to Robertson. I know, said Robertson. The Premier duly asked for the support of Robertson, his strongest ally within the Right. Robertson avoided an answer by saying he needed to talk to the General Secretary and get his views. When Robertson contacted Thistlethwaite, in puzzlement as to why he was going along with this reach for power, Thistlethwaite deflected the question by appealing to Robertson for his support.

Robertson was unconvinced. He had been unconvinced of the merits of the move before he arrived. He was unconvinced by the arguments he had heard. Robertson wanted to save Rees from himself, holding not a shade of doubt that the use of the powers to sack Tripodi would bring down Rees very soon after. He argued it was not too late not to proceed. Thistlethwaite countered that he was locked in, he must have the support of the group. Union leaders, wholly unimpressed by what they were being asked to vest in a premier who they regarded as from the Left, demanded to know when Thistlethwaite first knew of the plan. Thistlethwaite answered that his knowledge was very recent. These officials knew Thistlethwaite well. They did not believe his denial. His authority within the faction depended on absolute trust. His answer had forfeited that trust. Evidence of his much earlier knowledge was not long in emerging. Not that it mattered there and then: the Right was disinclined to humiliate their own man in the party office or to end the Rees leadership by denying him the authority he was seeking. That way was madness.

Preceding the Premier's address was a slide show of Rees' life narrated by Rees. The show eliminated the blue smoke and triumphalism. The media, side on, had to leave their seats to get a sense of the Premier's delivery and the reactions. The beginning of the Premier's address was still a long time distant. A vice president offered a welcome of unctuous vacuity. The enthusiasm of the greeting was effectively forfeited. To the managers of spin standing along the wings it was decidedly odd that this extended introduction had been allowed to destroy the theatre of the Premier's arrival.

After some powerful recitations of where the state was heading, Rees took the course unexpected. The government would legislate to ban donations from developers, the government would require all lobbyists to resign from its boards, all meetings between government officials and developers would be formal and minuted. Having set the mood, Rees made his plea:

> I come before you today to seek the same authority [as
> Rudd to appoint ministers]. Not after an election victory.
> But in order to win one. I seek this authority for one reason,
> and one reason alone: so that Labor leaders, present and
> future, can appoint Cabinets in which the people of New
> South Wales have confidence. My friends, I do not ask this
> lightly. I simply stand before you, trusting that you
> understand what I seek and the reasons why I seek it. I want
> to lead a party that upholds the same high standards as
> when Labor's journey first began. A party built on the
> age-old values of: unity, discipline, integrity and respect.

Some time during the request for the power to appoint and dismiss, the delegates realised they were present at a momentous occasion.

On the stage, surrounded by his colleagues, Rees could almost hear the MPs reaching for their Blackberries. When he finished he could see, in the faces of those who would look at him, that some were deeply angry. So were many of the Right delegates on the floor. Ending a sweetheart relationship with corporate donors was just as threatening to the Right's view of a proper world. No longer would MPs good at extracting funds surplus to their own campaign requirements be able to use finance to wield influence with fellow MPs and with the machine. Union donations could come within a future ban.

During the lunch break, the Right caucus of conference delegates met. Tony Burke MP (speaking with the authority of the Prime Minister) and John Robertson (loyal soldier) supported granting those powers to the leader. There was plenty of anger expressed. When the secretary of the shop assistants' union voiced his opposition, the General Secretary knew the proposition was on a dangerous salient. Kristina Keneally came to his aid by speaking in support. The motion was carried on the voices, a begrudging approval. Thistlethwaite had carried off brinksmanship that was breathtaking. Not even Graham Richardson at the height of his power would have contemplated a coup of those proportions, however secret and sensitive, without acquainting John Ducker and Paul Keating of every nuance of what was in the offing. Thistlethwaite had to know there were going to be consequences for him.

Word was abroad that Tripodi, Macdonald and another were for dismissal. Robertson warned Rees of the consequences of sacking Tripodi. In the end, Tripodi's offence was that he had been too publicly loyal, a loyalty that claimed a lot of media attention as if all that held up the Rees leadership was the ongoing support. That the assertion was largely correct did not make it tolerable. The perception shackled the Premier with impotence, a leader ultimately dependent on one who was held in poor regard by the electorate. Rees was resolute with Robertson, as he was with all those urging caution – a legion of genuine friends. Rees was determined to let the consequences fall however they might.

Back at Conference immediately after lunch, Thistlethwaite moved an amendment to the ALP Rules to grant the parliamentary leader the authority Rees sought. The debate was quiet. The passion had been expended at that earlier meeting. The resolution passed with only minor opposition, though three Right unions abstained and some officials absented themselves from the hall. Morris Iemma, at home with his family, watched his phone light up as of old.

Eighteen days

It is a short walk from the Entertainment Centre to the ALP office in downtown Sussex Street. Wedderburn had asked for a meeting with Thistlethwaite, Foley and Rees so that the authors of an unsettled state of affairs might consider where they were and where they would be. At 5:30 the four met in the General Secretary's office. The principal task was confirming the course of action – the dismissal of Tripodi and Macdonald. Who would tell Tripodi, given that Tripodi had cause to believe that his loyalty to Rees had been total? On the stage, in the aftermath of the announcement, Tripodi had not considered the Premier's intentions were either immediate or personal. Thistlethwaite agreed to contact Tripodi ahead of the Premier's call.

Rees went his own way. The other three went to the factional dinners. At the Right's gathering, Thistlethwaite and Wedderburn spoke some more. Tripodi now knew that the Premier wanted to see him. Not much imagination was required to know the business at hand. Wedderburn was insistent that Rees own the removals.

The next morning Rees called Tripodi and Macdonald and demanded their resignations. Another reshuffle came to pass. Immediately, he detected that the temperature of the sea had changed. The question for Rees was not how quickly the animosity reached boiling point but how long it stayed there. He was soon aware that key figures on the Right who usually regarded each other with nought but enmity had put enmity aside. He had united the Right against himself. Still, even now, with the Right overwhelmingly alienated and wanting to move against Rees, there would be no move until and unless Thistlethwaite endorsed the challenge.

The ALP President and the leaders of the major Right-wing unions began preparing the General Secretary for a change of mind. Bernie Riordan had become increasingly insistent that Rees had to go. The events of Conference ensured that the anti-Rees forces would no longer take no for an answer from the General Secretary. The machine was divided on who might be the replacement, a matter which had served the preservation of Rees. That identity did not now matter. The winner could emerge in the course of the execution. Whomever, she or he would be a member of the Right.

Only two candidates were credible. Frank Sartor, an MP since 2003 and minister from his first day – until sacked by Rees, was deeply unhappy on the backbench. Sartor was a focal point for anti-Rees feeling that was separate to the Obeid-Tripodi grouping, hitherto acquiescent to the Rees leadership, now bridling. In modern Labor it was no longer a handicap to have once stood against the endorsed Labor candidate at a general election, as had Sartor in an earlier incarnation. Carr had made Sartor's career possible by ensuring he was imposed on the electorate of Rockdale.

Kristina Keneally, an MP since the same year as Sartor, was the Minister for Planning. She is a native of the United States, uncommonly attractive, intellectually bright. In recent months, she had emerged as a contender, speculation not a matter she had discouraged. Keneally won her seat courtesy of a centralised selection ballot. She had come a long way since her woeful performance at the 2008 Annual Conference. (John Della Bosca was not taken seriously except by himself.)

Before anyone could launch a bid, there was the matter of getting the General Secretary to see where his duty lay. In conversations that became more explicit, Thistlethwaite came to understand that he could not long remain in the position. The difference between a departure in glory and something different required his open disowning of Rees, after which he would have to deploy the full authority of his office to compel the Right MPs as a bloc against the Premier. In the genome of every Right-wing ALP official is the memory of the fate of the General Secretary in 1976 who fell foul of the faction: that General Secretary returned from an overseas trip to find his resignation typed and the locks to the ALP office changed.

When exactly Thistlethwaite dropped Rees is not clear. Nor is it clear that a single conversation or moment caused his decision. One view is that Bernie Riordan threatened him with a choice between a parliamentary career and oblivion. Another is that the Right's MPs told Thistlethwaite they were moving against Rees with or without machine backing. Either circumstance, if either happened, could have been a bluff. Whatever the final impetus, conscious of the consequences of having kept secret his prior knowledge of the Rees' announcement at conference, Thistlethwaite decided to back the moves. Foley had taken parental leave on 30 November to be present for the arrival of his third child. Foley was essentially absent as the challenge against Rees came to pass. The Thistlethwaite switch ended the relationship of Foley and Thistlethwaite.

Gatherings of Right-wing MPs, meetings of chance and friendship as much as design, were addressing the new landscape. A consensus formed among those doubtful about taking out another leader that the bomb was going off whatever they did.

It was Wednesday, 2 December when Thistlethwaite called on Rees. They met in the Premier's office in Parliament House just after Question Time, Wedderburn present. Sitting on the lounges, Thistlethwaite indicated that it was getting tough, Right support for Rees was collapsing, his troops wanted to move. He and Arbib had fought for a delay. Rees asked Thistlethwaite directly whether he was himself sticking. The answer was yes. At no time did Thistlethwaite look Rees in the eye to state he was withdrawing his personal support. Thistlethwaite departed the room on the understanding of Rees and Wedderburn that the Premier and the General

Secretary were going to keep calling people to see if the situation was beyond rescue. Instead, Rees learned, Thistlethwaite set up camp elsewhere in Parliament House. From here, according to Rees, he was calling MPs from the Right to acquaint them with the new realities and what was expected of them – a matter of concentrating many minds on polling. The message was a proven winner: your sole hope of surviving is to shift to a new leader.

Later that Wednesday, Thistlethwaite attended a meeting in Tripodi's office where the mood for change was palpable. Present were Riordan, Tripodi, Obeid and Keneally. The group could not agree on a candidate, which meant they had not acquiesced to the view – being pushed hard by Thistlethwaite and Riordan – that Sartor was the one. They did agree that only one Right-wing candidate could go forward to the full Caucus, at which all members of the Right would be bound to vote for him – or her. For the Right to assert a binding vote would mean that the effective decision on the leadership would be made by them and them alone. A formal petition signed by the requisite number of Caucus members caused a special Caucus to be convened on the morrow.

At some point in this sequence, around 6:15 that evening, Thistlethwaite called Rees on his mobile to acquaint him with the news. The Right would be moving in the morning. In a cold, determined tone Rees, as Wedderburn listened, stated he was not impressed: at no time did you give me an inkling you had dropped your support. Rees told Wedderburn he felt as if he had been taken to a cul-de-sac and shot in the back of the head. The phone call delivered total awareness of what was happening and the objective hopelessness of his situation.

Thistlethwaite spent that evening in his office at party headquarters, with Riordan present for some of the time. Robertson was invited to Sussex Street, as a person of influence who needed strict corralling for the next 24 hours. Robertson arrived around 8:30 and departed at 9:50. To Thistlethwaite he asked a good question: do you have the numbers for Sartor? No. Have you talked to anyone? I am working on it. The machine cajoled Robertson to be a loyal member of the faction. Robertson gave no commitment and went home. Phone calls and discussions occupied the members of the parliamentary Labor party while the two Houses continued with their business. Rees reached every person of reason within the Right. He discovered they would stick with what the faction decided, regardless of personal doubts, Robertson included.

As he faced the rest of that evening, Rees was as calm as Iemma had been at the end. Nathan Rees was not emotional, not surprised, not shell-shocked. A formal notification that he was gone for all money was just another day in the office. Rees, more than anyone, appreciated the relentless pressure upon Thistlethwaite. In the privacy of his mind, Rees was capable of extending residual sympathy.

Execution

Rees began the final day of his leadership with a press conference. He and his staff thought long and hard about what he might say. The line taken came of the instant; wrapping it in words took a while longer. Having decided against a studied silence, the contents of what Rees felt compelled to say will enjoy a long afterlife:

> I will not hand the government of New South Wales over to Obeid, Tripodi or Sartor. Should I not be premier by the end of this day, let there be no doubt in the community's mind, no doubt, that any challenger will be a puppet of Eddie Obeid and Joe Tripodi. That is the reality. That is the choice at stake today. The decision now lies in the hands of my Caucus colleagues.

Word of his words spread rapidly. Many from the Right were livid he had so deliberately poisoned the chalice from which his successor would have to sip. There was shock at the audacity of it all. It was always unlikely such an assault would swing a vote, very likely the assault would confirm intentions. Rees felt the better for saying what needed saying. He had convened a morning Cabinet in the

Governor Macquarie Tower in the hope that distance from Parliament might encourage sober reflection. It was another occasion for straight talking from him.

The Right caucus met in the aftermath of the press conference. Its only business was the leadership. Not everyone agreed that Rees was terminal. In a caucus of 47 – one MP was absent – the opponents of the spill numbered 15. The spill motion was endorsed and, having been endorsed, was binding on all members of the Right. There was too much danger in an open contest against an incumbent premier. Nominations were invited for the candidate that the Right would put forward. Keneally and Sartor nominated. Sartor had cause to believe he would win – even unto the last moments he had pledges from those who would vote against him. Sartor had declined to commit to the return of Macdonald, a condition of Obeid's support. Believing that the government could win the next election only with a credible Cabinet, Sartor effectively forfeited the leadership. Sartor won back his reputation in the Labor Party by losing the leadership. Obeid and Tripodi were solid in their support of Keneally. They needed to be. Keneally won 25–22.

No breathless hush on the Close that morning. The meeting of the Parliamentary Labor Party lacked majesty, a scurvy affair reflective of the work at hand. A spill was moved by the two Right-wing ministers Rees had sacked. Consistent with the view that the leadership was private property returning to its owners, a motion of no confidence was introduced without speeches in support. That is, the gravest measure in the law of organisation did not warrant an argument. The movers muttered: 'The motion speaks for itself'. Carmel Tebbutt spoke with immense power against its passage. Throughout the Rees premiership she had been mentioned as an alternative. Not once had she encouraged that course. Finally and selflessly she renounced her own prospects.

The spill passed. The second ballot proceeded. The first leadership ballot in the New South Wales parliamentary Labor Party in 36 years. Keneally stood against Rees and won 47–21. It is worth noting that the Rees vote plus the Right votes against a spill would have constituted a majority. Such are the consequences of concentric binding. Rees had discovered, as had Iemma, that the majority group within the Right controlled the Caucus: 25 dictated to 70.

With the ballot announced, Rees stood in the leader's place and pledged his loyalty. The result ended an experience akin to waiting for an axe to fall. He returned to his office where the staff had assembled in the conference room. All were present. He warned them not to be too nice or he would lose it. After the speeches, he departed the building to the *Verandah Bar* in Elizabeth Street. He returned, in full possession of his senses, to start packing. Rees pondered that at no time did any of the plotters visit him for a discussion.

Morris Iemma departed the scene and did not thereafter make any public comment. He became seriously ill, for one fearful day within two hours of death. The grace of his departure from politics reminded people of his many good qualities. Iemma could have been the most significant Labor leader of modern times if he had demanded the end of union control of his party. A Labor leader will one day take that position, likely perish in the trying, but the anomaly of union control will not long survive a sustained assault by a parliamentary leader who proclaims the need to return the party to its membership. Leaving intact the union protection racket, while demolishing the rights of affiliates to play a role in ALP policy, would have resulted in the worst of all worlds. In 2010 Iemma became a Trustee of the Sydney Cricket Ground – the ninth Premier of New South Wales so honoured and the 15th party leader. Being a Trustee is compensation enough for anyone.

John Watkins watched his seat of Ryde fall to the Liberal Party in a landslide. After Ryde, no marginal Labor seat was beyond losing. Watkins gave sterling service to achieving public understanding of Alzheimer's. Michael Costa resigned from Parliament without sentiment. Too young to collect a pension, he wrote a column in the *Australian* and otherwise let his views be known. He wrote very well, largely adhering to a focus on what had gone wrong with the ALP. Reba Meagher disappeared without political trace.

Karl Bitar had an untroubled time as National Secretary. He came into his kingdom in the service of a federal parliamentary leader who was adept at learning the grabs that emerged from focus groups, equally adept at reciting those grabs word perfect as and when required. Bernie Riordan remained President, unchallenged. John Robertson took on several portfolios. His quiet competence took him below the radar. The party expected Robertson to seek a seat in the Legislative Assembly in the fullness of time. Graham Wedderburn, denied the Senate, returned to the private sector.

Nathan Rees remained a Member of the Legislative Assembly. He did not seek Cabinet office. He will recontest his safe seat of Toongabbie in 2011, after which he can expect to play a major role in whatever the ALP has then become. After his volley on the morning of his fall, he did not make another statement critical of the Premier who had replaced him.

The fall of Nathan Rees had a collateral casualty in Matt Thistlethwaite, whose position in the party office had become untenable. The strikes against him were fatal: inability to admit to the truth of how long he had known of Rees' plans for selecting the ministry; backing the loser for the Right's endorsement to replace Rees. Unlike Iemma and Rees, who had lost the confidence of the General Secretary, the lack of trust between Thistlethwaite and the new Premier was going to be a problem for the General Secretary. The Right had no appetite for another killing pre-Christmas. In mid-February 2010, the secretaries of the Right-wing unions took lunch in a private room in the *Golden Century* Chinese restaurant in Sussex Street, a gathering sufficiently intimate that all could be seated around the one circular table. Also invited were Matt Thistlethwaite and the assistant secretary, Sam Dastyari, age 27. In the week preceding, Thistlethwaite had received an offer too good to refuse – number two spot on the ALP Senate ticket. It was an offer he had helped float. The offer came with the endorsement of Mark Arbib and Bernie Riordan. The night before and that morning, Thistlethwaite talked the matter through with close colleagues and former mentors. At lunch Thistlethwaite announced his acceptance. Being placed in the Senate was unusual punishment. Now there was no spot for Wedderburn.

Electricity warrants consideration as a personality in its own right. The Plan B proposals for sale won the approval of the ALP and the government without any debate. No sale has taken place. Nor will a sale take place in the life of this government. The global financial crisis reduced the ranks of potential buyers. The plenitude of concessions won by the unions drove down the price of what assets were on offer. The prices exacted by the Kennett government in the 1990s look like windfalls today, on a par with the first prices for broadband spectrum. The fond hopes of Carr in 1997 and Iemma in 2007 were not within cooee of anything any longer out there.

Epilogue: Does party membership matter?

The Rudd government was the first federal Labor government with no meaningful connection to the Labor Party. A parliamentary leadership – courtesy of the taxpayers – enjoys a dominating public presence, unlimited travel, a standing army of MPs, a larger army of well-paid staffers, furnished offices in every capital city, computers, telephones and postage and stationery. Public funding of election campaigns and donations from the corporate sector have rendered unimportant the contributions of cash and energy from unions and party members. Electors are reached by direct mail and electronic mail. The letterbox delivery of the candidate's pamphlet is decidedly old hat. Local campaigns are not run locally and are local only in the sense that any deviations from the central message are authorised to the last comma. The organisation of the modern political party does not require a presence below, not even at election times – except perhaps for the odd photo opportunity.

Modern Labor operates in accordance with an axiom: a parliamentary leader sustained by good opinion polls will prevail on all matters, including decisions contrary to party policy. Where Morris Iemma had failed in New South Wales, Anna Bligh, Premier of Queensland, succeeded. She persuaded the Queensland ALP Conference to approve the sale of a wide range of public assets so as to overcome a shortage of finance. Her arguments were no more or less compelling (or specious) than those put by Morris Iemma but Bligh was a winner riding high in the polls. Resistance in the party folded abjectly and without honour. Within a short time, Bligh was struggling in the polls. A similar exercise a few months later would certainly have failed.

Kevin Rudd and his inner group succeeded in guiding every moment of the ALP's National Conference of 2009. They determined speakers, speaking times, even whether amendments were to be moved. A group of four, funded by the taxpayer, was in charge of vetting amendments prior to their tabling. A leadership group has presumed to determine preselections for any seat that Labor has a chance of winning wherever the local membership might select a candidate unacceptable to that group. Rudd, even as Opposition Leader with the right trajectory in the polls, could demand the expulsion of a union leader for rough language – and have his demand met. He could rub out potential candidates for preselection confident that his wishes would be met by those craven to impress him.

Modern politics exists in an age that is post-belief. A shortfall in the taxation revenues available to a government will occasion the same response from both sides of politics – sell assets, reduce staff, slash services. The once Labor belief in higher taxation and reinvestment in public assets for future dividends is seen as preposterously out of date.

Modern political leadership has lost the capacity to persuade. As parties have abandoned beliefs as a means of developing a coherent program for action in office, government has become increasingly episodic, reactive and poll-driven. Focus groups and qualitative polling have become more important in determining policy settings than the formal decisions of parties in conference. Conviction is a useful prelude to convincing others that what you are advocating is good for the nation. The absence of conviction is soon apparent to an electorate that is entitled to be sceptical. Cynicism has become self-perpetuating. Courage goes missing. When a government invests more effort in planning the announcement than the content of the announcement, it is a bad government.

Does a party need a membership to win an election? No. The Labor Party, the destroyer of a class system based on grandees and clients, has evolved into a party of grandees' clients. There is no one in a position of influence in any Labor government who is prepared to act as the members' champion. The National Executive has become a tyranny to enforce the will of the factional leaderships which control it lock, stock and dividend stream. The members of the Labor Party are without a voice in their own party.

Does a party need a membership at all? No. The principal purpose of a party membership was to provide the credentials for preselection for a seat in parliament. Those credentials were the only means of gaining the right to nominate as a candidate. Not any more. Parliamentary leaderships can and will anoint who enters the ranks of parliament. A government riding high in the polls will demand and receive protection from internal criticism. It will receive the removal of all dissent from the public view of party gatherings. A leader can demand and will receive the expulsion of those who make public utterances that embarrass the leader.

Unable to make a meaningful contribution to an organisation they have joined, members will walk away. It is scarcely a comfort to note that the malaise of the Australian Labor Party is the plight of social democratic parties everywhere. Nor that every voluntary association in Australia is suffering from a lack of commitment, or a dependence on a tiny number of stalwarts. People will not remain in a political party in which their only function is to offer applause for the leadership, not unless such people possess ambitions to gain paid employment in the gift of the party. Membership of the ALP is ageing, the numbers are falling. They will not recover. The leadership has no interest in supporting a revival. Election victories have proven the party does not need a membership.

Appendix A

NSW ALP branches closed 1999–2009

Argenton–Edgeworth	Casino	Doonside
Auburn North	Castlecrag	Drummoyne
Avoca	Castlereagh	East Hills
Beaconsfield	Cecil Hills	East Nowra
Berkshire Park	Claremont Meadows	Evans Head
Belmont	Cobar	Figtree
Bodalla–Narooma	Coledale–Scarborough	The Forest
Bonalbo	Colongra Bay	Glebe
Bourke	Coniston	Glenn Innes
Braidwood	Coolah	Goonellabah
Brisbania	Coonabarabran	Grahamstown
Bundarra	Coonamble	Gundagai
Camdenville	Corowa	Hamilton
Camperdown	Cowra	Hawks Nest
Canley Vale	Croydon North	Heathcote
Carrington	Culburra	Helensburgh

Holbrook
Hume
Hurstville
Illawong–Alfords
  Point
Imlay
Jesmond–North
  Lambton
Jugiong
King
Kingsgrove
Kotara
Lakemba
Lambton–East
  Lambton
Lilyfield
Liverpool East
Llandilo
Manilla
Mannering
  Park–Vales Point

McCallums Hill
Molong
Mortdale
Mt Kembla
Narara–Niagara
  Park
Narrabri
Narranderra
Nine Mile Beach
Noraville
Oatley
Padstow Heights
Peak Hill
Pelican
Quirindi
Rankin Park–Elemore
  Vale
Sawtell
Stewart
Summerland Point
Sussex Inlet

Tanilba
Temora
Tenterfield
Tighes Hill
Tuggerawong
Turramurra
Walgett–Lightning
  Ridge
Wallamba Day
Wamberal Day
Waterloo
Wauchope
Windang
Wingate Day
Wingham
Worrigee Day
Wyong–North
  Gosford
Yanco

(Total: 101)

(Source: ALP records. Compiled by Luke Foley.)

Appendix B

NSW ALP financial membership 2002–09

Year	Total financial members
2002	19 609
2003	17 550
2004	17 591
2005	17 341
2006	16 508
2007	16 454
2008	17 199
2009	15 385

There were 15 385 financial members of the NSW ALP at September 2009, comprising:

Category A (employed or in receipt of income): 4090

Category B (members of affiliated unions): 2444

Category C (students, retired, home duties, pensioners, unemployed): 8400

Life members: 451.

There are fewer than 7000 ALP members in New South Wales who work for a living. There are 3 621 800 people in the New South Wales workforce: only one fifth of one per cent of working people belong to the Labor Party.

Category B membership – ALP members who are members of ALP affiliated unions – is under 2500. That is slightly over one-half of 1 per cent of the 384 000 members of trade unions who are affiliated with the NSW ALP through their union.

NSW Labor's trade union affiliates represent a bare 10 per cent of the NSW workforce. This proportion is declining.

(Source: ALP membership records. Researcher: Luke Foley.)

Appendix C

Delegates to NSW ALP Annual Conference, May 2008

Body	Votes
AIMPE (marine and power engineers)	1
AMIEU (meat industry)	7
AMWU (metal workers)	27
ASU (services)	12
AWU (Australian Workers Union)	27
CEPU (communications, postal)	15
CFMEU (construction, forestry, mining)	26
CPSU (Commonwealth public service)	8
ETU (electrical trades)	20
FSU (financial services)	15
HSU (health services)	39
LHMU (liquor, hospitality, miscellaneous)	32
MEAA (media, entertainment, arts)	5
MUA (maritime)	3
NUW (National Union of Workers)	18
RTBU (rail, tram, bus)	17

(*cont.*)

Body	Votes
SDA (shop assistants)	71
TCFU (textile, clothing, footwear)	4
TWU (transport)	42
USU (municipal)	38
Unions subtotal	**427**
Federal Electorate Councils (49 x 3 delegates each)	147
State Electorate Councils (93 x 2 delegates each)	186
Federal Parliamentary Labor Party	16
State Parliamentary Labor Party	16
Young Labor	16
Policy Committee office holders	45
(15 Committees x 3 office holders)	
Party subtotal	**426**
Administrative Committee	34
Total	**887**

(Source: ALP records. Researcher: Michael Samaras.)

Sources

My principal source for this book was my own diaries. Entries in my diaries are based on conversation, quiet listening with unobtrusive, very occasional prods. As soon as practical, you reduce your memory of a conversation to writing. Speed is of the essence in recording your memories. Other conversations will confirm, enhance or undermine an earlier conversation. Honest witnesses to the same event will have a different recall, what was central to one was peripheral to others. Participants told the author what was happening, conscious the information would be reported without attribution except when express permission was granted

A rough, unintended draft of this book appeared in the *Newsletter of the Southern Highlands Branch* of the Australian Labor Party over six issues between March and October 2008. Over the course of 164 issues (as of July 2010), the *Newsletter* has regularly carried essays on the governance of the ALP. That body of work was my most useful resource when it came to considering the events of 2008. The *Newsletter* essays on Labor's crisis of 2008 appeared as follows:

'Forget Wollongong: privatisation of electricity is the potential government killer' (no 138, March 2008)

'Who decides: a conundrum worthy of Thomas More and Archbishop Cranmer' (no 139, April 2008)

'Conference asserts its sovereignty' (no 140, May 2008)

'NSW Government defies Annual Conference' (no 141, June 2008)

'A study of leadership changes in NSW Labor, 1939–2005' (no 143, August 2008)

'Iemma falls' (no 145, October 2008).

I have drawn on two addresses to the NSW Fabians: 'Could Chifley win preselection today?' (20 April 2005) and 'What happened to the Left? It died.' (20 September 2008).

Formal interviews took place with Morris Iemma, Nathan Rees, Luke Foley, Graeme Wedderburn and many others who do not wish to be named. Carl Green, Lynda Voltz and Mick Veitch rendered invaluable assistance by verifying events and dates.

Books

Troy Bramston (ed), *The Wran Era* (Federation Press 2006)

Ernie Chaples, Helen Nelson and Ken Turner (eds), *The Wran Model: Electoral Politics in New South Wales, 1981 and 1984* (OUP 1985)

VG Childe, *How Labour Governs: A study of workers' representation in Australia* (MUP 1964)

David Clune and Ken Turner (eds), *The Premiers of New South Wales*, 2 vols (Federation Press 2006)

Chris Cuneen, *William John McKell: Boilermaker, Premier, Governor-General* (UNSW Press 2000)

Bruce Duncan, *Crusade or Conspiracy: Catholics and the anti-communist struggle in Australia* (UNSW Press 2001)

Maurice Duverger, *Political Parties: Their organization and activity in the modern state* (University Paperbacks 1964)

Michael Easson (ed), *McKell: The achievements of William McKell* (Allen & Unwin 1988)

HV Evatt, *Australian Labour Leader: The story of WA Holman and the Labour movement* (Angus & Robertson 1940)

LF Fitzhardinge, *William Morris Hughes: A political biography*, 2 vols (Angus & Robertson 1964 and 1979)

Graham Freudenberg, *Cause For Power: The official history of the New South Wales Branch of the Australian Labor Party* (Pluto 1991)

Jim Hagan and Ken Turner, *A History of the Labor Party in New South Wales 1891–1991* (Longman 1991)

Michael Hogan, *Local Labor: A history of the Labor Party in Glebe 1891–2003* (Federation Press 2004)

Michael Hogan (ed), *Labor Pains: Early conference and executive reports of the Labor Party in New South Wales*, vols 1–3, 1892–1917 (Federation Press 2006)

Michael Hogan and David Clune (eds) *The People's Choice: Electoral politics in 20th century New South Wales*, 3 vols (NSW Parliament 2001)

P Loveday, AW Martin & Patrick Weller, 'New South Wales' in P Loveday, AW Martin & RS Parker (eds), *The Emergence of the Australian Party System* (Hale & Iremonger 1977)

Judy Mackinolty (ed), *The Wasted Years? Australia's Great Depression* (Allen & Unwin 1981)

Raymond Markey, *The Making of the Labor Party in New South Wales 1880–1900* (UNSW Press 1988)

Robert Michels, *Political Parties: A sociological study of the emergence of leadership, the psychology of power and the oligarchic tendencies of organization* (Dover 1959)

Andrew Moore, *The Secret Army and the Premier* (UNSW Press 1989)

Robert Murray, *The Split: Australian Labor in the fifties* (Cheshire 1970)

Bede Nairn, *Civilising Capitalism: The Labor movement in New South Wales 1870–1900* (ANU Press 1973)

— *The 'Big Fella': Jack Lang and the Australian Labor Party 1891–1949* (MUP 1986)

Heather Radi and Peter Spearritt (eds), *Jack Lang* (Hale and Iremonger 1977)

LL Robson, *The First AIF: A study of its recruitment 1914–1918* (MUP 1970)

Andrew Scott, *Fading Loyalties: The Australian Labor Party and the working class* (Pluto 1991)

Andrew Scott, *Running On Empty: 'Modernising' the British and Australian labour parties* (Pluto 2000)

Mike Steketee and Milton Cockburn, *Wran: An unauthorised biography* (Allen & Unwin 1986)

Articles

Troy Bramston and Rodney Cavalier, 'What happened in 1973', *Southern Highlands Branch ALP Newsletter* (no 144, September 2008)

Rodney Cavalier, 'The Australian Labor Party at Branch Level: Guildford, Hunters Hill and Panania Branches in the 1950s', in Whitlam et al (eds), *A Century Of Social Change: Labor History Essays*, vol 4 (Pluto Press 1992)

Michael Easson, 'The McKell Model', *Southern Highlands Branch ALP Newsletter* (no 147, December 2008)

Luke Foley, 'The impact of corporate cash on ALP membership and the health of the party', interview, ABC TV *Four Corners*, transcript reproduced in *Southern Highlands Branch ALP Newsletter* (no 140, May 2008)

David Marr, 'Suburban son rises', *Sydney Morning Herald*, 17 March 2007

Michael Samaras, 'Annual Conference: Supreme and illegitimate', *Southern Highlands Branch ALP Newsletter* (no 147, December 2008)

Unpublished sources

David Clune, 'The Labor government in New South Wales 1941–1965: A study in longevity in government', unpublished PhD thesis, University of Sydney, 1990.

Index

Meagher, Reba 107, 109, 127, 140, 148, 155, 181–2
media
  coverage of NSW state politics and privatisation issue 95–9, 114, 117, 119, 120–2, 125, 127, 132, 133, 137–8, 139, 145, 169
  hostility to legitimacy of Labor's internal governance 117–18
  industrial reporters 96–7
  and undermining of Rees 159, 169
Menzies, Robert Gordon 24, 40
ministerial selection 169, 173–4
ministerial staff 49–50, 142
Murphy, Lionel 27

Nairn, Bede 11–12
National Conference (ALP)
  control of 2009 conference by Rudd 184
  critics of 90–1
  implications of control of conference 31
  proportion of union delegates reduced 31
  union control of conference floor 31–2
  see also Labor Electoral League NSW Annual Conference; NSW Labor Annual Conference – May 2008; NSW Labor Annual Conference – November 2009
National Executive (ALP) 114–15, 136–7, 161
National Party, blue collar vote 34
Newspoll 138, 139
NSW Labor
  Caucus independence 51
  defiance of the Pledge 3–4, 10
  Federal intervention 14
  first government 7
  general secretary's position 70, 71–4, 75–8
  meeting of Parliamentary party in December 1973 28–9
  nature of factions 11–12
  in opposition 23–5
  power to elect leader returned to Caucus 19
  preselection 55–6
  State Executive 12
  victory in 2007 election 66, 67–70
NSW Labor Annual Conference – May 2008
  agenda behind vote on electricity privatisation 89
  Bitar–Foley amendment 111

conference calls Iemma government to account 116–18
contest over electricty 58
convened at Sydney Convention Centre 94–5
critics of 90–1
debate on privatisation 103–14
delegates 191–2
formalities and rituals 99–100
Premier's address by Iemma 100–3
presidential address 99–100
Robertson amendment 105, 111–14
Rudd's address 114, 115
Thistlethwaite amendment 103–4, 105
union control of conference 85
unrepresentative nature of conference 85, 134
vote on Robertson amendment 113–14
NSW Labor Annual Conference – November 2009
  authority granted to parliamentary leader to select ministers 175
  convened at Sydney Entertainment Centre 171–5
  meeting of Right faction 172
  premier's address 172, 173–4
NSW Labor branches
  closures 47, 187–8
  financial membership 2002–2009 189–90
  membership 47–8, 189–90
NSW Labor Left faction
  death of 39–47
  face test in Parliament 122
  opposition to electricity privatisation 85, 93
  'Socialist Left' 45
  sub-groups 147–8
  support for Unsworth 29
NSW Labor Right faction
  and appointment of ministers 171–3
  balkanises 158
  Catholic-based 47
  Centre Unity 38
  challenge to Rees 176
  control of Caucus 181
  management 72–4
  meeting to 'execute' Iemma 149, 150–1
  moves to depose Rees 176–9
  myth regarding Wran's leadership 25–30
  opposition to electricity privatisation 85
  and role of general secretary 76, 77
  'Trogs' and 'Terrigals' 158
  undermining of Rees 158–60

Saluszinsky, Imre 144
Santamaria, BA 10
Sartor, Frank 127, 129, 157, 176, 178, 180, 181
Scully, Carl 30, 64–5
Secord, Walt 125
Sheldon, Tony 104
Simpson, Jack 97
socialism
    and the ALP 11–12, 39–40
    death of 42
solidarity principle 2–4, 9
Spigelman, Jim 153
State Corporations Act 114
state governments
    privatisation 80
    restrictions imposed on Labor premiers 3
Stewart, Kevin 28
Stewart, Tony 63–4
Storey, John 15
Swancott, Neal 97

tax reform 34
Tebbutt, Carmel 125, 127, 147, 153
Theodore, Ted 14, 16
Thistlethwaite, Matt 92, 103–4, 105, 160–1, 164, 170–1, 175, 176–9, 182–3
three mines policy (uranium) 41–2
trade unions
    amalgamations 53
    death of union culture in the workplace 33
    lose of social relevance 34–7
    unaffiliated to the ALP 35–6
trade unions (affiliated with ALP)
    control of ALP 13, 33, 36, 52–3, 58
    control of ALP Conference 31–2, 85
    decline 53
    formation of ALP 1
    host body of political class 52–4
    membership 32–3
    and political operatives 52–3
    private baronies 73
    representation at ALP Conference 14–15, 31

sense of possession of the ALP 6
spoils culture at ALP conferences 31–2
Transport Workers' Union 73
Tripodi, Joe 65, 127, 141, 145, 146, 149, 151, 155, 156, 165–6, 178, 180, 181
Trotskyists 10
Turnbull, Malcolm 41
Turner, Ray 97

Union of Australian Workers 73
Unions NSW
    negotiations over electricity privatisation 82
    opposition to electricity privatisation 85–6
universal manhood suffrage 29
Unsworth, Barrie 29, 75, 83, 90, 93, 103–6, 108, 147, 157
Unsworth Committee 83–4
uranium policy 41
Usher, Lorraine 105

Veitch, Mike 142
Voltz, Lynda 120

Watkins, John 99, 106, 107, 146–7, 180–1
Wedderburn, Graeme 125, 163–5, 170–1, 177, 182
Wells, Fred 96
Wentworth, Billy 41
West, Graham 148–9
West, Ian 120
Westerway, Peter 76
Whelan, Paul 155
Whitlam, Gough 48, 60, 74–5, 153
Whitlam government 25, 48
Williams, Michael 104
workplace culture
    death of union culture 33
    and union membership prior to 1970s 32–3
Wran, Neville 21, 25–9, 64, 68, 74, 101, 103, 112, 155, 156–7
Wran government 112

Australian Encounters series

Cambridge University Press Australia, in partnership with the National Centre for Australian Studies at Monash University, presents *Australian Encounters*. Combining original scholarly research and elegant, accessible prose, this series engages with important Australian issues that span current society, politics, culture, economics and historical debates. It brings new thinking and fresh perspectives to these issues that are so vital to Australian society.

Series editor

Dr Tony Moore is Lecturer in Media and Communications and Director of the National Centre for Australian Studies, Monash University.

Forthcoming titles in the Australian Encounters series

Curtin's Empire

James Curran

Senior Lecturer in history at the University of Sydney argues for a revision of the popular myth of wartime Prime Minister John Curtin as an opponent of the British Empire.

The Importance of Being Innocent

Joanne Faulkner

UNSW philosopher Joanne Faulkner critiques the construction of children as innocent and asks what it means for children who fail to meet these idealistic criteria.